NEW ENGLAND
KNITS

NEW ENGLAND KNITS

KNITS

TIMELESS KNITWEAR
WITH A **MODERN TWIST**

Cecily Glowik MacDonald AND Melissa LaBarre

INTERWEAVE.
interweavestore.com

Editor Anne Merrow

Technical Editor Karen Frisa

Cover and Interior Design Karla Baker

Photography Sadie Dayton

Illustrations Ann Sabin Swanson

Stylist Marci Duarte

Hair and Makeup Audrey Berman

Production Katherine Jackson

Interweave Press LLC
201 East Fourth Street
Loveland, CO 80537
interweavestore.com

Printed in China by Imago.

Library of Congress Cataloging-in-Publication Data

MacDonald, Cecily Glowik.
   New England knits : timeless knitwear with a modern
twist / Cecily Glowik MacDonald and Melissa LaBarre.
      p. cm.
   Includes index.
   ISBN 978-1-59668-180-4
   1. Knitting--Patterns. 2. Sweaters--New England. 3.
Dress accessories--New England. I. LaBarre, Melissa.
II. Title.
   TT825.M1534 2010
   746.43'2041--dc22

                              2009045235

10 9 8 7 6 5 4 3 2 1

This book is dedicated to Ethan and Robyn.
We owe you some really nice sweaters.

Acknowledgments

We would like to wholeheartedly thank Tricia Waddell for believing in our idea. Without her support and enthusiasm, this book would not have been possible. We will always be grateful.

Thanks to Anne Merrow, our lovely editor, for her patience and knowledge. As new authors, we took full advantage of both. And thanks to all the folks at Interweave who've enthusiastically supported us, more than we could have ever imagined.

We will always be grateful to Pam Allen, who cheered us on, offered advice, and went out of her way to help make this book match our vision. Her kindness will never be forgotten.

Big thanks to our families and friends, for their love and support. We couldn't have done this without them. They stuck with us, pretended to be interested in knitting, and not one of them rolled their eyes at the mention of this book, ever. Without the love, hugs, food, and humor they offered us, we surely would have drowned in yarn.

We would like to thank the yarn companies who donated yarn for the projects: Classic Elite Yarns, Vermont Organic Fiber Company, Fairmount Fibers/Manos del Uruguay, Kelbourne Woolens/The Fibre Co., Berroco, Tahki/Stacy Charles, Louet, Shibui, Muench/GGH, JCA, and Bijou Bison.

We are also grateful to our guest designers and native New Englanders, Kate Gagnon Osborn, Kristen TenDyke, Cirilia Rose, and Carrie Hoge, for sharing their talents with us.

Last but not least, thank you to our amazing knitter, Amanda Hosmer. Her perfect stitches saved our wrists from ruin.

Happy knitting!

Melissa and Cecily

welcome to
NEW ENGLAND

It seems entirely fitting that the idea for this book was born on a perfect fall day. One October morning, we left our homes in wool cardigans and hats. As the day went on, the hats came off and the cardigans hung open until the sun went down. It was then that we found ourselves scrambling for woolly layers again. Handknits get lots of use here; the weather gives us many opportunities for that.

As knitters and native New Englanders, it's hard not to be inspired by our surroundings when thinking about what we want to knit. That afternoon, while talking about what we wanted to knit next, we realized that we had strikingly similar visions for a perfect New England wardrobe.

Composed of six states, New England offers inspiration in many forms. With winter approaching, we were drawn to cold weather first and brainstormed knits for snowy days—warm pieces that would keep out the brisk cold air on the shortest days. As five of the region's six states border the ocean, the New England coast inspired us, too, but not in the beach-going sunbathing way. Instead, we thought of the colors and cool coastal winds found here. We pictured walks in the woods in crisp fall weather and days spent in the park enjoying the midst of spring.

We were drawn to transitional-weather clothes. New England is notorious for sudden weather shifts, so we thought of cardigans and pieces for layering. You know that favorite cardigan, the one you reach for again and again, that you throw on instead of a coat on a crisp fall day? We hope you'll find one of those among this collection: classic pieces with a modern detail or two that you'll enjoy making and want to keep forever.

And so *New England Knits* was born. Thinking of the farms scattered across the region and the fiber-producing animals that reside here, we chose natural fibers like wool. Its ability to repel water and provide warmth made it the perfect canvas for the projects we envisioned.

We shared our plans with a few designers who hail from New England and asked them to join us and contribute designs that felt like perfect New England knits. We think you'll find that they've succeeded.

around
THE TOWN

New England is full of quaint little towns with old brick buildings that have been transformed to house modern restaurants and shops. A walk through cobblestone streets can be a daylong adventure where history is intermingled with hip boutiques and cafés. The garments in this section are designed for a day spent strolling around one of these towns. These pieces are a little polished and can go from a day of sightseeing to a romantic evening dinner. A lovely cardigan with sweet button details at the neck, a skirt dressed up with a bit of lace at the hem, and a soft kerchief with delicate bead details are just a few of the items that will take you around the town.

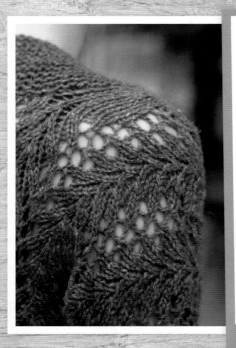

hampton
CARDIGAN

DESIGNER
Cecily Glowik MacDonald

This cardigan in super-soft wool and yak is suitable for more than one season. Working the sweater in one piece, from the back over the sleeves to the fronts, allows the lace pattern to progress uninterrupted. Garter stitch at the cuffs and lapels plus a large hook-and-eye closure set off the warm lace beautifully.

finished size

36 (39½, 43½, 47, 51)" (91.5 [100.5, 110.5, 119.5, 129.5] cm) bust circumference, closed; cardigan shown measures 36" (91.5 cm).

YARN

DK (Light #3).

shown here: Bijou Basin Ranch (50% yak, 50% Cormo; 150 yd [137 m]/56 g): heathered gray brown, 6 (7, 8, 8, 9) skeins.

NEEDLES

U.S. size 7 (4.5 mm): 29" (73.5 cm) circular (cir). Adjust needle size if necessary to obtain the correct gauge.

NOTIONS

Markers (m); tapestry needle; one large hook-and-eye closure.

GAUGE

19 sts and 22 rows = 4" (10 cm) in vine lace patt.

Cardigan

Back

Using the long-tail method (see Glossary), CO 85 (94, 103, 112, 121) sts. Do not join. Work 4 rows in garter st.

NEXT ROW: (WS) Work 2 sts in St st, place marker (pm), work Row 1 of Vine Lace chart to last 2 sts, pm, work 2 sts in St st.

Cont in patt until piece measures 15 (14½, 14, 13½, 13)" (38 [37, 35.5, 34.5, 33] cm) from CO, ending with a RS row.

Sleeve Cast-on

NEXT ROW: (WS) Using the cable method (see Glossary), CO 54 sts at beg of row. Slide sts to other end of needle and turn work so that RS is facing, then attach a new strand of yarn to beg of RS row. Using the cable method, CO 54 sts, break yarn—193 (202, 211, 220, 229) sts.

Slide sts to other end of needle. With WS facing, work 2 sts in St st, pm, work Vine Lace Patt to last 2 sts (removing markers as you come to them), pm, work 2 sts in St st.

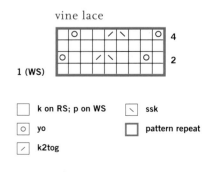

vine lace

k on RS; p on WS   ssk

o yo   □ pattern repeat

/ k2tog

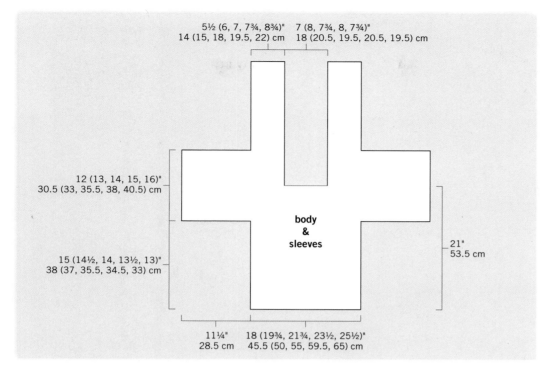

5½ (6, 7, 7¾, 8¾)"
14 (15, 18, 19.5, 22) cm

7 (8, 7¾, 8, 7¾)"
18 (20.5, 19.5, 20.5, 19.5) cm

12 (13, 14, 15, 16)"
30.5 (33, 35.5, 38, 40.5) cm

body
&
sleeves

21"
53.5 cm

15 (14½, 14, 13½, 13)"
38 (37, 35.5, 34.5, 33) cm

11¼"
28.5 cm

18 (19¾, 21¾, 23½, 25½)"
45.5 (50, 55, 59.5, 65) cm

Work even in patt until piece measures 6 (6½, 7, 7½, 8)" (15 [16.5, 18, 19, 20.5] cm) from sleeve CO, ending with a RS row.

Shape Neck

Work 74 (74, 83, 83, 92) sts in patt as established, pm, work 6 (8, 4, 8, 4) sts in St st, attach a new strand of yarn, BO center 33 (38, 37, 38, 37) sts, work 6 (8, 4, 8, 4) sts in St st, pm, work in vine lace patt to last 2 sts, work 2 sts in St st—80 (82, 87, 91, 96) sts rem each side. Work even in patt as established until piece measures 12 (13, 14, 15, 16)" (30.5 [33, 35.5, 38, 40.5] cm) from sleeve CO, ending with a RS row.

Sleeve Bind-Off

NEXT ROW: (WS) BO 54 sts for left sleeve, work in patt to end of left front; work 26 (28, 33, 37, 42) sts in patt for right front, BO next 54 sts for right sleeve—26 (28, 33, 37, 42) sts rem each side.

With RS facing, break yarn and reattach to right front sts.

NEXT ROW: (RS) Work 2 sts in St st, pm, work in patt as established to last 2 sts of left front, pm, work 2 sts in St st.

Cont working both sides in patt as established until piece measures 14½ (14, 13½, 13, 12½)" (37 [35.5, 34.5, 33, 31.5] cm) from sleeve BO, ending with a WS row. Work in garter st for 4 rows. BO all sts loosely kwise.

Finishing

Block piece to measurements.

Collar

With RS facing and beg at bottom of right front, pick up and knit (see Glossary) 80 sts evenly spaced along right front edge, 30 (35, 34, 35, 34) sts evenly spaced across back neck, and 80 sts evenly spaced along left front edge—190 (195, 194, 195, 194) sts total. Work even in garter st for 3" (7.5 cm), ending with a RS row. With WS facing, BO all sts loosely kwise.

Cuffs

With RS facing, pick up and knit 42 (47, 53, 58, 63) sts along end of sleeve. Work even in garter st for 2¼" (5.5 cm), ending with a RS row. With WS facing, BO all sts loosely kwise.

With yarn threaded on a tapestry needle, sew side and sleeve seams. Sew hook and eye to edges of opposite lapels about 9½" (24 cm) from bottom edges.

chelsea SKIRT

DESIGNER
Cecily Glowik MacDonald

This skirt has a delicate lace border that peeks out from under the edge, worked in a soft contrasting-color yarn that echoes the tweedy flecks of the main skirt. The herringbone stitch pattern adds structure and detail to the shape, and a row of buttons up the side creates a strong and slimming line.

finished size

32 (37¼, 42½, 48)" (81.5 [94.5, 108, 122] cm) circumference below waist-band, buttoned, and 21" (53.5 cm) long, including lace trim; skirt shown measures 32" (81.5 cm).

YARN

Worsted (Medium #4) and lace (Lace #0).

shown here: Classic Elite Portland Tweed (50% wool, 25% alpaca, 25% viscose; 120 yd [110 m]/50 g): #5058 ruby red (MC), 7 (8, 8, 9) balls.

Classic Elite Silky Alpaca Lace (70% alpaca, 30% silk; 460 yd [421 m]/50 g): #2477 forget me not (blue; CC), 1 ball.

NEEDLES

U.S. sizes 5, 6, and 7 (3.75, 4, and 4.5 mm): 29" (73.5 cm) circular (cir). Adjust needle size if necessary to obtain the correct gauge.

NOTIONS

Two (two, three, three) 30 yd [27.5 m] spools of elastic sewing thread; nine ⅝" (1.5 cm) buttons; matching sewing thread and sewing needle; tapestry needle.

GAUGE

21 sts and 26 rows = 4" (10 cm) in St st with MC on smallest needle.

Stitch Guide

herringbone pattern
(multiple of 7 sts + 1)

ROWS 1 AND 3: (WS) Purl.

ROW 2: *K2tog, k2, RLI (see Glossary), k2; rep from * to last st, k1.

ROW 4: K1, *k2, RLI, k2, k2tog; rep from * to end.

Rep Rows 1–4 for patt.

seed stitch
(multiple of 2 sts + 1)

ROW 1: K1, *p1, k1; rep from * to end.

Rep Row 1 for patt.

lace trim pattern
(multiple of 13 sts)

ROW 1 AND ALL WS ROWS: K2, purl to last 2 sts, k2.

ROW 2: Sl 1, k3, yo, k5, yo, k2tog, yo, k2—15 sts.

ROW 4: Sl 1, k4, sl 1, k2tog, psso, k2, [yo, k2tog] 2 times, k1—13 sts rem.

ROW 6: Sl 1, k3, ssk, k2, [yo, k2tog] 2 times, k1—12 sts rem.

ROW 8: Sl 1, k2, ssk, k2, [yo, k2tog] 2 times, k1—11 sts rem.

ROW 10: Sl 1, k1, ssk, k2, [yo, k2tog] 2 times, k1—10 sts rem.

ROW 12: K1, ssk, k2, yo, k1, yo, k2tog, yo, k2—11 sts.

ROW 14: Sl 1, [k3, yo] 2 times, k2tog, yo, k2—13 sts.

Rep Rows 1–14 for patt.

Skirt

With largest needle and MC, CO 197 (225, 253, 281) sts. Do not join. Work in herringbone patt (see Stitch Guide) until piece measures 8" (20.5 cm) from CO, ending with a WS row. Change to middle-size needle. Cont in patt until piece measures 15" (38 cm) from CO, ending with a WS row. Change to smallest needle and St st. Work 2 rows even.

NEXT ROW: (RS) Dec 2 sts randomly spaced across row, using k2tog—2 sts dec'd.

Rep dec row every row 15 more times, using p2tog for WS row decs and distributing decs randomly across fabric—165 (193, 221, 249) sts rem. *Note:* In order for the decs not to show, they must be worked in different spots on every row.

Work 4 rows even in St st.

Attach elastic sewing thread. With MC and elastic held tog, work in k1, p1 rib for 1½" (3.8 cm), ending with a WS row. BO all sts in rib.

Finishing

Block piece to measurements.

Buttonhole Band

With smallest needle, MC, and RS facing, beg at CO edge, pick up and knit (see Glossary) 109 sts

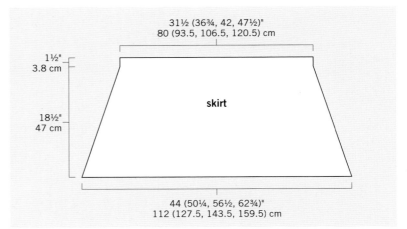

31½ (36¾, 42, 47½)"
80 (93.5, 106.5, 120.5) cm

1½"
3.8 cm

18½"
47 cm

skirt

44 (50¼, 56½, 62¾)"
112 (127.5, 143.5, 159.5) cm

along side edge of skirt to BO edge. Work even in seed st (see Stitch Guide) for 5 rows.

NEXT ROW: (RS; buttonhole row) Work 24 sts in patt, *yo, k2tog, work 8 sts in patt; rep from * to last 5 sts, yo, k2tog, work in patt to end.

Work 3 rows in seed st. BO all sts kwise.

Buttonband

With smallest needle, MC, and RS facing, beg at BO edge, pick up and knit 109 sts along side edge of skirt to CO edge. Work even in seed st for 3 rows. BO all sts kwise.

Lace Trim

With largest needle and CC, CO 13 sts. Work Lace Trim patt (see Stitch Guide) until piece measures same length as bottom of skirt. Leaving sts on needle (or placing on holder), block lace trim, then recheck fit around bottom of skirt. Adjust length if needed by working more rows or ripping back rows, then BO all sts. With sewing needle and matching thread, sew straight edge of edging to WS of skirt along lower edge so that most of edging is visible when skirt is worn.

Sew buttons to buttonband opposite buttonholes. Weave in loose ends.

ashfield
CARDIGAN

DESIGNER
Melissa LaBarre

This pretty and flattering top-down cardigan has a nipped-in waist and leaf lace front panels. With button tab closures and buttons on both fronts, the sweater can be customized by adding as many or as few buttons as you like and placing them to suit your taste. It's perfect for layering over a tank or T-shirt on a breezy day.

finished size

33½ (35, 40, 43, 45, 49, 54)" (85 [89, 101.5, 109, 114.5, 124.5, 137] cm) bust circumference, buttoned; cardigan shown measures 35" (89 cm).

YARN

Sportweight (Fine #2).

shown here: St-Denis Nordique (100% wool; 150 yd [137 m]/50 g): #5852 eggplant, 7 (8, 9, 10, 11, 12, 14) balls.

NEEDLES

U.S. size 4 (3.5 mm): 32" (80 cm) or longer cir and set of 4 or 5 dpn. U.S. size 3 (3.25 mm): cir. Adjust needle size if necessary to obtain the correct gauge.

NOTIONS

Markers (m; 4 in each of 2 colors); stitch holders or waste yarn; four ½" (1.3 cm) buttons; sewing needle and matching thread; tapestry needle.

GAUGE

23 sts and 36 rows = 4" (10 cm) in St st on larger needle.

15 sts of lace panel = 2¼" (5.5 cm) wide, after blocking.

Cardigan

With larger cir needle and using the long-tail method (see Glossary), CO 85 sts. Do not join.

Shape Neckline

ROW 1: (WS) Purl to end, then, using the backward-loop method (see Glossary), CO 4 sts—89 sts.

ROWS 2–4: Work in St st to end, then CO 4 sts—101 sts after Row 4 is complete.

ROWS 5 AND 6: Work in St st to end, then CO 16 sts—133 sts after Row 6 is complete.

ROW 7: P1, place marker (pm) for lace panel, p15, pm for lace panel, p10, pm for raglan, p14, pm for raglan, p53, pm for raglan, p14, pm for raglan, p10, pm for lace panel, p15, pm for lace panel, p1.

Shape Raglan

ROW 1: (RS; inc row) K1, work Left Lace chart to m, sl m, *knit to 1 st before raglan m, M1R (see Glossary), k1, sl m, k1, M1L (see Glossary); rep from * 3 more times, knit to m, work Right Lace chart to m, k1—8 sts inc'd.

ROW 2: Purl.

Rep last 2 rows 19 (21, 28, 30, 33, 39, 44) more times—293 (309, 365, 381, 405, 453, 493) sts.

Divide for Body and Sleeves

NEXT ROW: (RS) Work in patt to raglan m, remove m, place 54 (58, 72, 76, 82, 94, 104) sleeve sts onto holder, remove m, use the backward-loop method to CO 2 (2, 2, 4, 4, 4, 6) sts for underarm, pm, CO 2 (2, 2, 4, 4, 4, 6) sts for underarm, k93 (97, 111, 115, 121, 133, 143) back sts, remove m, place 54 (58, 72, 76, 82, 94, 104) sleeve sts onto holder, remove m, use the backward-loop method to CO 2 (2, 2, 4, 4, 4, 6) sts for underarm, pm, CO 2 (2, 2, 4, 4, 4, 6) sts for underarm, work in patt to end—193 (201, 229, 245, 257, 281, 309) sts rem for body.

Cont in patt, working St st and lace patt, until piece measures 2" (5 cm) from underarm, ending with a WS row.

Shape Waist

NEXT ROW: (RS; dec row) Work in patt to end of lace panel, k5, ssk, k1, k2tog, knit to side m, k43 (45, 52, 56, 59, 65, 72), ssk, k1, ssk, k1, k2tog, k1, k2tog, knit to 10 sts before lace panel m, ssk, k1, k2tog, work in patt to end—185 (193, 221, 237, 249, 273, 301) sts rem.

Work 3 rows even.

right lace

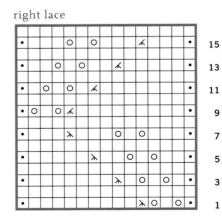

left lace

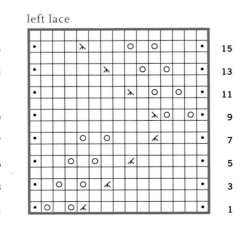

	k on RS; p on WS
•	p on RS; k on WS
○	yo
↗	k3tog
⅄	sssk
	pattern repeat

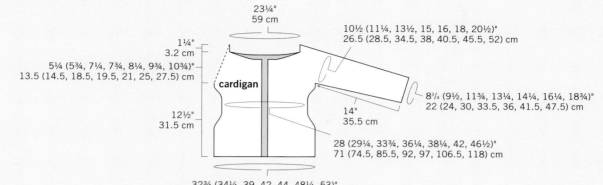

23¼"
59 cm

1¼"
3.2 cm

5¼ (5¾, 7¼, 7¾, 8¼, 9¾, 10¾)"
13.5 (14.5, 18.5, 19.5, 21, 25, 27.5) cm

cardigan

12½"
31.5 cm

10½ (11¼, 13½, 15, 16, 18, 20½)"
26.5 (28.5, 34.5, 38, 40.5, 45.5, 52) cm

8³/₄ (9½, 11¾, 13¼, 14¼, 16¼, 18¾)"
22 (24, 30, 33.5, 36, 41.5, 47.5) cm

14"
35.5 cm

28 (29¼, 33¾, 36¼, 38¼, 42, 46½)"
71 (74.5, 85.5, 92, 97, 106.5, 118) cm

32¾ (34¼, 39, 42, 44, 48¼, 53)"
83 (87, 99, 106.5, 112, 122.5, 134.5) cm

NEXT ROW: (RS; dec row) Work in patt to end of lace panel, k5, k3tog, knit to side m, k43 (45, 52, 56, 59, 65, 72), sssk (see Glossary), k1, k3tog, knit to 8 sts before lace panel m, sssk, work in patt to end—177 (185, 213, 229, 241, 265, 293) sts rem.

Purl 1 WS row.

Waist Ribbing

NEXT ROW: (RS) Work to end of lace panel, work in k1, p1 rib to next lace panel, work in patt to end.

Cont in lace and rib patt as established until rib measures 2" (5 cm), ending with a WS row.

NEXT ROW: (RS; inc row) Work to end of lace panel, k4, (knit into front, back, and front) of next 2 sts, knit to side m, k42 (44, 51, 55, 58, 64, 71), (knit into front, back, and front) of next 2 sts, k1, (knit into front, back, and front) of next 2 sts, work to 6 sts before lace panel m, (knit into front, back, and front) of next 2 sts, work in patt to end—193 (201, 229, 245, 257, 281, 309) sts.

Cont in St st and lace patt until piece measures 10½" (26.5 cm) from underarm, ending with a WS row.

Change to smaller cir needle and work in garter st for 2" (5 cm), ending with a WS row.

With RS facing, BO all sts pwise.

Sleeves

Place 54 (58, 72, 76, 82, 94, 104) held sleeve sts onto larger dpn. Beg at center of underarm, pick up and knit (see Glossary) 3 (3, 3, 5, 5, 5, 7) sts in CO sts, k54 (58, 72, 76, 82, 94, 104), pick up and knit 3 (3, 3, 5, 5, 5, 7) sts in CO sts—60 (64, 78, 86, 92, 104, 118) sts total. Pm and join for working in the rnd.

Work in St st until piece measures 6" (15 cm) from underarm.

NEXT RND: (dec rnd) K2, k2tog, knit to last 4 sts, ssk, k2—2 sts dec'd.

Rep dec rnd every 10th rnd 4 more times—50 (54, 68, 76, 82, 94, 108) sts rem.

Work even in St st until piece measures 12" (30.5 cm) from underarm.

Change to smaller dpn and work in garter st (purl 1 rnd, knit 1 rnd) for 2" (5 cm), ending with a purl rnd. BO all sts pwise.

Finishing

Collar

With RS facing and smaller cir needle, pick up and knit 133 sts evenly spaced around neck opening. Do not join. Work 10 rows in garter st. With WS facing, BO all sts kwise.

Buttonbands

With RS facing and smaller cir needle, pick up and knit 116 (119, 129, 133, 137, 146, 153) sts along right front edge (including collar). Work 6 rows in garter st. With WS facing, BO all sts kwise. Rep for left front edge.

Button Tab (make 2)

With smaller dpn, CO 5 sts. Do not join.

ROWS 1–4: Knit.

ROW 5: (buttonhole row) K1, k2tog, yo, k2.

ROWS 6–13: Knit.

ROW 14: Rep Row 5.

Knit 4 rows. BO all sts.

Block sweater to open up lace panels.

With sewing needle and thread, sew 2 buttons to each buttonband, sewing first button ½" (1.3 cm) from upper edge and second button about 2¼" (5.5 cm) below first.

Pass buttons through tab buttonholes.

Weave in loose ends.

auburn TOP

DESIGNER
Cecily Glowik MacDonald

This classic-feeling pullover, with a shawl collar to keep your neck warm, makes a perfect everyday sweater. The waist-shaping increases and decreases are worked toward the center of the sweater rather than hidden along the side seams. The visible darts resemble princess shaping, a slimming design that flatters a variety of figures.

finished size

35¼ (38¾, 42, 47¼, 50½)" (89.5 [98.5, 106.5, 120, 128.5] cm) bust circumference; sweater shown measures 35¼" (89.5 cm).

YARN
Worsted (Medium #4).

shown here: **Berroco Inca Gold** (80% merino, 20% silk; 122 yd [112 m]/50 g): #6415 terracotta, 9 (10, 10, 12, 12) hanks.

NEEDLES
U.S. size 6 (4 mm): 16" (40 cm) circular (cir). U.S. size 7 (4.5 mm): 24" (60 cm) cir and set of 4 or 5 double-pointed (dpn). Adjust needle size if necessary to obtain the correct gauge.

NOTIONS
Markers (m; 1 of one color and 4 of another); stitch holders or waste yarn; tapestry needle.

GAUGE
19 sts and 26 rows = 4" (10 cm) in St st on larger needle.

Body

With larger needle, CO 168 (184, 200, 224, 240) sts. Place marker (pm) and join for working in the rnd, being careful not to twist sts.

Work in k1, p1 rib for 2" (5 cm).

NEXT RND: Change to St st and pm for darts as foll: K21 (23, 25, 28, 30), pm, k42 (46, 50, 56, 60), pm, k42 (46, 50, 56, 60), pm, k42 (46, 50, 56, 60), pm, knit to end.

Shape Waist

NEXT RND: (dec rnd) [Work to 2 sts before m, ssk, work to next m, k2tog] 2 times, work to end of rnd—4 sts dec'd.

Rep dec rnd every 6th rnd 4 more times—148 (164, 180, 204, 220) sts rem. Work even in St st for 1" (2.5 cm).

NEXT RND: (inc rnd) [Work to 1 st before m, M1R (see Glossary), k1, work to next m, k1, M1L (see Glossary)] 2 times, work to end of rnd—4 sts inc'd.

Rep inc rnd every 10th rnd 4 more times—168 (184, 200, 224, 240) sts. Work even in St st (removing dart markers) until piece measures 15 (14½, 14, 13½, 13)" (38 [37, 35.5, 34.5, 33] cm) from CO, ending last rnd 5 (5, 5, 6, 7) sts before end of rnd.

Divide Front and Back

BO 10 (10, 10, 12, 14) sts, removing m for beg of rnd, k74 (82, 90, 100, 106) front sts, BO 10 (10, 10, 12, 14) sts, k74 (82, 90, 100, 106) back sts. Place front sts on holder or waste yarn.

Back

NEXT ROW: (WS) Purl.

Shape Armholes

NEXT ROW: (RS; dec row) K1, ssk, knit to last 3 sts, k2tog, k1—2 sts dec'd.

NEXT ROW: Purl.

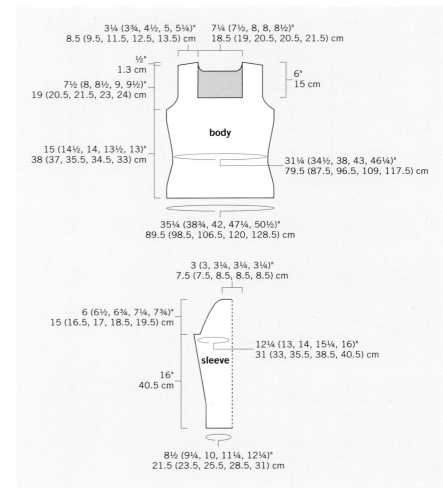

Rep last 2 rows 4 (4, 4, 6, 7) more times—64 (72, 80, 86, 90) sts rem. Work even until armholes measure 6½ (7, 7½, 8, 8½)" (16.5 [18, 19, 20.5, 21.5] cm), ending with a WS row.

Shape Neck

K17 (20, 23, 26, 27), attach a new strand of yarn, BO 30 (32, 34, 34, 36) sts, work to end—17 (20, 23, 26, 27) sts rem each side. Working both sides at the same time, work 1 WS row even.

NEXT ROW: (RS; dec row) Knit to 3 sts before neck BO, k2tog, k1; on second side, k1, ssk, knit to end—1 st dec'd each side.

Work last 2 rows once more—15 (18, 21, 24, 25) sts rem each side. Work even until armholes measure 7½ (8, 8½, 9, 9½)" (19 [20.5, 21.5, 23, 24] cm), ending with a WS row.

Shape Shoulders

BO 7 (9, 10, 12, 12) sts at beg of next 2 rows—8 (9, 11, 12, 13) sts rem each side. BO 8 (9, 11, 12, 13) sts at beg of foll 2 rows—no sts rem.

Front

Place 74 (82, 90, 100, 106) held front sts onto needle. With WS facing, attach yarn. Work as for back until armholes measure 2 (2½, 3, 3½, 4)" (5 [6.5, 7.5, 9, 10] cm), ending with a WS row.

Shape Neck

NEXT ROW: (RS) K15 (18, 21, 24, 25), attach a new strand of yarn, BO 34 (36, 38, 38, 40) sts, work to end—15 (18, 21, 24, 25) sts rem each side.

Working both sides at the same time, work even until armholes measure 7½ (8, 8½, 9, 9½)" (19 [20.5, 21.5, 23, 24] cm), ending with a WS row.

Shape Shoulders

BO 7 (9, 10, 12, 12) sts at beg of next 2 rows—8 (9, 11, 12, 13) sts rem each side. BO 8 (9, 11, 12, 13) sts at beg of foll 2 rows—no sts rem.

Sleeves

With dpn, CO 40 (44, 48, 54, 58) sts. Pm and join for working in the rnd, being careful not to twist sts.

Work in k1, p1 rib for 4" (10 cm).

NEXT RND: (inc rnd) K1, M1L, work to 1 st before m, M1R, k1—2 sts inc'd.

Rep inc rnd every 8th rnd 3 more times, then every 10th rnd 5 times—58 (62, 66, 72, 76) sts.

Work even until piece measures 16" (40.5 cm) from CO.

Shape Cap

Work to 5 (5, 5, 6, 7) sts before m, BO 10 (10, 10, 12, 14) sts, k1, ssk, knit to last 3 sts, k2tog, k1—46 (50, 54, 58, 60) sts rem. Turn work and purl 1 WS row.

NEXT ROW: (RS; dec row) K1, ssk, knit to last 3 sts, k2tog, k1—2 sts dec'd.

Rep dec row every RS row 3 (5, 4, 6, 7) more times—38 (38, 44, 44, 44) sts rem.

Work even until piece measures 6 (6½, 6¾, 7¼, 7¾)" (15 [16.5, 17, 18.5, 19.5] cm) from first dec row, ending with a WS row.

NEXT ROW: (RS) K1, *k3tog; rep from * to last st, k1—14 (14, 16, 16, 16) sts rem. BO all sts pwise.

Finishing

Block pieces to measurements. With yarn threaded on a tapestry needle, sew shoulder seams. Sew in sleeves.

Picot Edging

With smaller needle and beg at right edge of back neck BO, pick up and knit (see Glossary) 34 (36, 38, 38, 40) sts along back neck BO, 4 sts to shoulder seam, 25 sts along left front neck edge, 35 (37, 39, 39, 41) sts along center front, 25 sts along right front neck edge to shoulder, and 4 sts to back neck BO—127 (131, 135, 135, 139) sts.

NEXT ROW: Work picot edge as foll: BO 2 sts, *sl st on right needle to left needle, CO 1 st, BO 4 sts; rep from * to last 2 (3, 1, 1, 2) st(s), sl st on right needle to left needle, CO 1 st, BO 3 (4, 2, 2, 3) sts.

Collar

With smaller needle, CO 43 (45, 47, 47, 49) sts. Do not join. Work in k1, p1 rib until piece measures 22 (23, 24, 24, 25)" (56 [58.5, 61, 61, 63.5] cm) from CO, ending with a WS row. BO all sts in patt.

Sew BO edge of collar to left front edge of front neck BO. Sew CO edge of collar to right front edge of front neck BO, overlapping 2" (5 cm) with BO edge of collar. Sew selvedge edge of collar to sides and back of neck opening, easing to fit.

Sewing Set-in Sleeves

To ensure that set-in sleeves are set into the armhole correctly, first pin them into place. Start by pinning the center of the top of the sleeve cap to the shoulder seam, then line up and pin the bound-off underarm stitches of the sleeve to the bound-off underarm stitches of the body. This allows you to ease in and pin the sides of the cap and the sides of the armhole evenly before seaming.

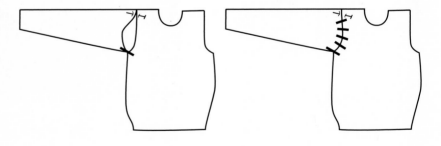

groveland
SATCHEL

DESIGNER
Cecily Glowik MacDonald

This roomy messenger-style bag gets its three-dimensional texture from a cable and bobble pattern that stands out even after fulling. The fulling process provides stability to the structured body and the doubled strap. The lining and custom buttons add a polished and unique finishing touch—choose fabric to contrast or coordinate with the yarn.

finished size

13" (33 cm) tall, 12" (30.5 cm) wide, and 4½" (11.5 cm) deep, excluding strap, after fulling.

YARN

Chunky (Bulky #5).

shown here: Debbie Bliss Donegal Chunky Tweed (100% wool; 109 yd [100 m]/100 g): #24 grass green, 4 hanks.

NEEDLES

U.S. size 9 (5.5 mm). Adjust needle size if necessary to obtain the correct gauge.

NOTIONS

Markers (m); cable needle (cn); tapestry needle; two 1⅛" (3 cm) buttons; sewing needle and thread; 32" x 17½" (81.5 x 44.5 cm) piece of lining fabric; 10½" (26.5 cm) square of lining fabric; 4¾" x 10" (12 x 25.5 cm) piece of cardboard for bag bottom.

GAUGE

14 sts and 20 rows = 4" (10 cm) in St st before fulling.

Stitch Guide

slip-stitch pattern
(multiple of 2 sts)

ROWS 1 AND 3: (WS) Purl.

ROW 2: (RS) K1, *sl 1 with yarn in front (wyf), k1; rep from * to last st, k1.

ROW 4: K2, *sl 1 wyf, k1; rep from * to end.

Rep Rows 1–4 for patt.

Back Panel

CO 50 sts.

SET-UP ROW: (WS) Work Cable chart, place marker (pm), work Bobble Vine chart, pm, work Cable chart.

WORK IN patt as established until piece measures 15" (38 cm) from CO, ending with a WS row.

NEXT ROW: (RS; turning row) [P5, p2tog, p6, p2tog] 3 times, p5—44 sts rem. Change to slip st patt (see Stitch Guide) and work even for 5" (12.5 cm), ending with a RS row.

NEXT ROW: (WS; buttonhole row) Work 7 sts in patt, BO 2 sts, work in patt to last 9 sts, BO 2 sts, work in patt to end—40 sts rem.

NEXT ROW: *Work in slip st patt to BO sts, use the backward-loop method (see Glossary) to CO 2 sts; rep from * once more, work in patt to end—44 sts.

Work even in patt until piece measures 6" (15 cm) from turning row, ending with a WS row. BO all sts.

Front Panel

CO 50 sts and work as for back panel until piece measures 15" (38 cm) from CO, ending with a WS row. BO all sts.

Strap

CO 18 sts. Work in slip st patt until piece measures 21" (53.5 cm) from CO, ending with a WS row.

cable

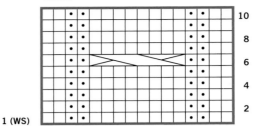

1 (WS)

bobble vine

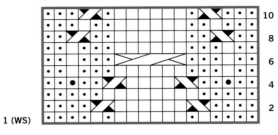

1 (WS)

☐	k on RS; p on WS
·	p on RS; k on WS
●	(knit into front, back, and front) of next st, turn; p3, turn; k3, turn; p3, turn; sl 1, k2tog, psso
☐	pattern repeat

sl 1 st onto cn, hold in back, k1, p1 from cn

sl 1 st onto cn, hold in front, p1, k1 from cn

sl 3 sts onto cn, hold in back, k3, k3 from cn

sl 4 sts onto cn, hold in front, k4, k4 from cn

NEXT ROW: (RS; dec row) K1, ssk, work in patt to last 3 sts, k2tog, k1—2 sts dec'd.

NEXT ROW: Purl.

Rep last 2 rows 2 more times—12 sts rem. Change to St st. Work even until piece measures 44" (112 cm) from CO, ending with a WS row. Change to slip st patt.

NEXT ROW: (RS; inc row) K1, M1 (see Glossary), work in patt to last st, M1, k1—2 sts inc'd.

NEXT ROW: Purl.

Rep last 2 rows 2 more times—18 sts. Work even in slip st patt until piece measures 65" (165 cm) from CO, ending with a RS row. BO all sts in patt.

Finishing

Block pieces to measurements.

With yarn threaded on a tapestry needle, use mattress st (see Glossary) to sew edges of St st portion of strap tog. With RS's facing out, align CO edge of strap with center of CO edge of back panel. Sew side of strap to back panel along bottom and side of back panel to turning row. Sew CO edge of strap to BO edge, making sure strap is not twisted. Sew strap to back panel along bottom and side as for first side. Sew front panel to sides of strap opposite back panel.

Fulling

Full piece by hand or machine until sts are tightened, but still visible. (Full a test swatch first to see how yarn will react.)

Fold flap to front. Sew buttons to front opposite buttonholes.

Lining

Fold larger piece of lining fabric in half widthwise with RS tog. Using a ½" (1.3 cm) seam allowance, sew side seams. At lower edge of lining, sew a seam 2¼" (5.5 cm) from each corner to form triangles **(Figure 1, below)**. Tack points of triangles to bottom of lining **(Figures 2 and 3)**. Turn upper edge of lining under ½" (1.3 cm). With WS of lining against WS of bag, insert lining into bag. Sew top of lining to upper edge of bag.

Bottom Insert

Fold smaller piece of lining fabric in half with RS tog. Using a ½" (1.3 cm) seam allowance, sew along one short side and one long side to form a pocket. Turn pocket RS out. Insert cardboard into pocket. Sew end closed using a ½" (1.3 cm) seam allowance. Insert into bottom of bag.

LINING CONSTRUCTION

figure 1

figure 2

figure 3

northampton
NECKERCHIEF

DESIGNER
Cirilia Rose

This kerchief is a classic square shawl shape, but worked on a smaller scale that can be folded into a triangle and tied or pinned for a sweet little accessory and a toasty neck. A lace edging, yarnover increases, and beaded detail provide a simple but polished finish.

finished size
About 30" (76 cm) square, after blocking.

YARN

Fingering (Super Fine #1).

shown here: Berroco Ultra Alpaca Fine (50% wool, 30% alpaca, 20% nylon; 433 yd [396 m]/100 g): #1293 spice-berry mix (bronze; A), #1284 prune mix (purple; B), and #1282 boysen-berry mix (red; C), 1 skein each.

NEEDLES

U.S. size 5 (3.75 mm): set of 5 double-pointed (dpn) and 16" (40 cm) circular (cir). Adjust needle size if necessary to obtain the correct gauge.

NOTIONS

U.S. size F/5 (3.75 mm) crochet hook; beading needle; 344 size 6° (size E) glass seed beads in gold or amber; 1 locking ring marker (m); 8 markers; digital scale (optional).

GAUGE

21 sts and 36 rnds = 4" (10 cm) in St st, after blocking.

Stitch Guide

place bead (pb)

Slide bead up to needle. Sl 1 pwise with yarn in front (wyf). Bead will sit on the small float of yarn in front of slipped st.

Kerchief

A Section

With A and using Emily Ocker's method (see Glossary), CO 12 sts. Divide sts evenly onto 4 dpn. Join for working in the rnd, being careful not to twist sts. Tighten center by tugging on original yarn loop tail.

SET-UP RND: Needle 1: K1, placing locking marker (pm) on this st to mark beg of rnd, pm for patt, yo, k1, yo, pm, k1; Needle 2: K1, pm, yo, k1, yo, pm, k1; Needle 3: K1, pm, yo, k1, yo, pm, k1; Needle 4: K1, pm, yo, k1, yo, pm, k1—20 sts.

Knit 1 rnd.

RND 1: *K1, sl m, yo, knit to m, yo, sl m, k1; rep from * to end—8 sts inc'd.

RND 2: Knit.

Rep Rnds 1 and 2 thirty-three more times, then work Rnd 1 once more—300 sts; 73 sts between markers. *Note:* Change to cir needle when there are too many sts to work comfortably on dpn.

B Section

Using beading needle, string 140 beads onto B.

NEXT RND: (bead rnd) With B, [k1, sl m, k2, *pb (see Stitch Guide), k1; rep from * to 1 st before m, k1, sl m, k1] 4 times.

With B, work Rnds 1 and 2 (from A section) 15 times, then work Rnd 1 once more—428 sts; 105 sts between markers; B section measures about 3½" (9 cm).

C Section

Using beading needle, string 204 beads onto C. With C, rep bead rnd (from B section). With C, work Rnds 1 and 2 (from A section) 3 times—452 sts; 111 sts between markers. Work lace edging as foll:

RND 1: **K1, sl m, yo, [k1, yo] 2 times, *[ssk] 2 times, sl 2 as if to k2tog, k1, p2sso, [k2tog] 2 times, [yo, k1] 5 times, yo; rep from * to 13 sts before m, [ssk] 2 times, sl 2 as if to k2tog, k1, p2sso, [k2tog] 2 times, [yo, k1] 2 times, yo, sl m, k1; rep from ** to end.

RNDS 2–4: Knit.

Rep last 4 rnds 2 more times.

RND 13: Purl.

RND 14: Knit.

RND 15: Purl.

BO all sts as foll: *Using the cable method (see Glossary), CO 1 st, BO 3 sts, sl st from right needle to left needle; rep from * until all sts have been bound off.

Finishing

Weave in loose ends. Block to measurements.

knit with a friend

With the introduction of Ravelry and knitting groups and knitting-based events taking place all over the world, knitting has become a very social activity. This scarf was conceived to be knitted with a friend—the yarn requirements provide enough yardage to make two matching kerchiefs. Use a gram scale to divvy up the yarn prior to knitting to make sure each of you will have enough to complete the project.

greylock
TUNIC

DESIGNER
Melissa LaBarre

This light tunic has a tank-dress shape and contrast-color accents for a figure-flattering fit. The rows of ruching at the waist are an eye-catching detail that's fun to work. The piece is perfect for layering over pants for a walk on a cool day; the length offers extra protection against the cold.

finished size

34¼ (38¼, 42¼, 46¼, 50¼)" (87 [97, 107.5, 117.5, 127.5] cm) bust circumference; tunic shown measures 34¼" (87 cm).

YARN

DK (Light #3).

shown here: Rowan Purelife Organic Wool Naturally Dyed (100% organic wool; 137 yd [125 m]/50 g): #607 onion (tan; MC), 7 (8, 10, 11, 12) balls, and #604 tannin (brown; CC), 1 ball.

NEEDLES

U.S. size 6 (4 mm): 24" (60 cm) and 40" (100 cm) circular (cir). U.S. size 5 (3.75 mm): 16" (40 cm) cir and set of 4 or 5 double-pointed (dpn). Adjust needle size if necessary to obtain the correct gauge.

NOTIONS

6 markers (m; one in a contrasting color for beg of rnd); stitch holders or waste yarn; tapestry needle.

GAUGE

22 sts and 32 rows = 4" (10 cm) in St st on larger needle.

Tunic

With shorter larger cir needle and MC, CO 220 (242, 264, 286, 308) sts. Place marker (pm) in contrasting color and join for working in the rnd, being careful not to twist sts.

NEXT RND: K110 (121, 132, 143, 154), pm, knit to end.

Work in St st until piece measures 2½ (2½, 3, 3, 3)" (6.5 [6.5, 7.5, 7.5, 7.5] cm) from CO.

NEXT RND: (dec rnd) *K8, ssk, knit to 10 sts before m, k2tog, k8; rep from * once more—4 sts dec'd.

Rep dec rnd every 8th rnd 3 more times, then every 10th rnd 5 times—184 (206, 228, 250, 272) sts rem.

Knit 2 rnds.

NEXT RND: (dec rnd) *K8, ssk, k2, ssk, knit to 14 sts before m, k2tog, k2, k2tog, k8; rep from * once more—176 (198, 220, 242, 264) sts rem.

Waist

RND 1: Purl.

RND 2: Knit.

RND 3: Purl.

Change to longer larger cir needle.

RND 4: (inc rnd) *K1f&b (see Glossary); rep from * to end—352 (396, 440, 484, 528) sts.

RNDS 5–12: Knit.

Change to shorter larger cir needle.

RND 13: *K2tog; rep from * to end—176 (198, 220, 242, 264) sts rem.

Rep Rnds 1–13 once more, then work Rnds 1–3 again. Knit 1 rnd.

Bust

NEXT RND: (inc rnd) *K8, k1f&b, knit to 9 sts before m, k1f&b, k8; rep from * once more—4 sts inc'd.

Rep inc rnd every 4th rnd 2 more times—188 (210, 232, 254, 276) sts.

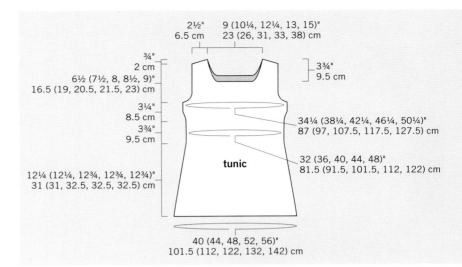

2½"
6.5 cm

9 (10¼, 12¼, 13, 15)"
23 (26, 31, 33, 38) cm

¾"
2 cm

6½ (7½, 8, 8½, 9)"
16.5 (19, 20.5, 21.5, 23) cm

3¾"
9.5 cm

3¼"
8.5 cm

3¾"
9.5 cm

tunic

34¼ (38¼, 42¼, 46¼, 50¼)"
87 (97, 107.5, 117.5, 127.5) cm

32 (36, 40, 44, 48)"
81.5 (91.5, 101.5, 112, 122) cm

12¼ (12¼, 12¾, 12¾, 12¾)"
31 (31, 32.5, 32.5, 32.5) cm

40 (44, 48, 52, 56)"
101.5 (112, 122, 132, 142) cm

Work even in St st until piece measures 2" (5 cm) from last inc rnd.

Divide for Front and Back

NEXT ROW: BO 4 (6, 6, 8, 8) sts, knit to m; place next 94 (105, 116, 127, 138) sts on holder for back—90 (99, 110, 119, 130) sts rem for front.

NEXT ROW: (WS) BO 4 (6, 6, 8, 8) sts, purl to end—86 (93, 104, 111, 122) sts rem.

Shape Armholes

NEXT ROW: (RS; dec row) K1, k3tog, work in St st to last 4 sts, sssk (see Glossary), k1—4 sts dec'd.

Rep dec row every RS row 1 (1, 1, 2, 2) more time(s)—78 (85, 96, 99, 110) sts rem.

Work even in St st until armholes measure 3½ (4½, 5, 5½, 6)" (9 [11.5, 12.5, 14, 15] cm), ending with a WS row.

Shape Neck

NEXT ROW: (RS) K20, attach a new strand of yarn and BO 38 (45, 56, 59, 70) sts, knit to end—20 sts rem each side.

Work both sides at the same time. Work 1 WS row.

NEXT ROW: (RS; dec row) Work to 4 sts before BO sts, sssk, k1; on second side, k1, k3tog, knit to end—2 sts dec'd each side.

NEXT ROW: Purl.

Rep last 2 rows once more—16 sts rem each side.

NEXT ROW: (RS; dec row) Work to 3 sts before BO sts, ssk, k1; on second side, k1, k2tog, knit to end—1 st dec'd each side.

Rep last dec row every RS row once more—14 sts rem each side.

Work even in St st until armholes measure 6½ (7½, 8, 8½, 9)" (16.5 [19, 20.5, 21.5, 23] cm), ending with a WS row.

Shape Shoulders

BO 3 sts at each armhole edge 2 times—8 sts rem each side. BO all sts.

Back

With RS facing, join MC. BO 4 (6, 6, 8, 8) sts at beg of next 2 rows—86 (93, 104, 111, 122) sts rem. Shape armholes as for front. Work even until armholes measure 4½ (5½, 6, 6½, 7)" (11.5 [14, 15, 16.5, 18] cm), ending with a WS row. Shape neck as for front. Work even until armholes measure 6½ (7½, 8, 8½, 9)" (16.5 [19, 20.5, 21.5, 23] cm), ending with a WS row. Shape shoulders as for front.

Finishing

Sew shoulder seams.

Bottom Edging

With RS facing, CC, longer larger cir needle, and beg at center back, pick up and knit (see Glossary) 220 (242, 264, 286, 308) sts around lower edge. Pm and join for working in the rnd.

Purl 1 rnd.

NEXT RND: (inc rnd) *K1f&b; rep from * to end—440 (484, 528, 572, 616) sts.

Knit 3 rnds.

NEXT RND: (dec rnd) *K2tog; rep from * to end—220 (242, 264, 286, 308) sts rem.

Purl 1 rnd.

Knit 1 rnd.

BO all sts pwise.

Neck Edging

With RS facing, CC, smaller cir needle, and beg at center back of neck, pick up and knit 33 (36, 42, 44, 49) sts to left shoulder, 79 (86, 97, 100, 111) sts across front to right shoulder, and 33 (36, 42, 44, 49) sts to center back—145 (158, 181, 188, 209) sts total. Pm and join for working in the rnd. Purl 1 rnd. BO all sts kwise.

Armhole Edging

With CC, dpn, and RS facing, beg at center of underarm, pick up and knit 52 (61, 65, 70, 74) sts to shoulder, then 52 (61, 65, 70, 74) sts to underarm—104 (122, 130, 140, 148) sts total. Pm and join for working in the rnd. Purl 1 rnd. BO all sts kwise.

Weave in loose ends.

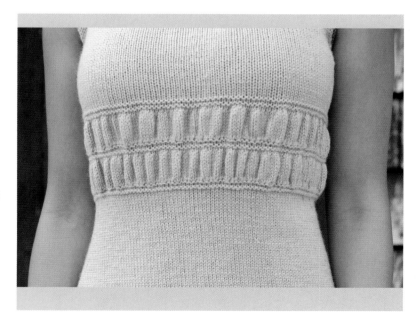

fairfield SWEATER

DESIGNER
Cecily Glowik MacDonald

The top of this comfortable slouch-neck cardigan is knitted from cuff to cuff. A skirt-style bottom is worked separately from the bottom up and embellished with a stem-stitch pattern, then joined to the top half. A bit of embroidery and whimsical buttons for closure and decoration add a finishing touch.

finished size

34 (38, 42, 46, 50)" (86.5 [96.5, 106.5, 117, 127] cm) bust circumference, buttoned; cardigan shown measures 34" (86.5 cm).

YARN

Worsted (Medium #4).

shown here: Classic Elite Kumara (85% extra fine merino, 15% camel; 128 yd [117 m]/50 g): #5706 Perkin's mauve, 9 (10, 11, 12, 13) skeins.

NEEDLES

U.S. sizes 7, 8, and 9 (4.5, 5, and 5.5 mm). Adjust needle size if necessary to obtain the correct gauge.

NOTIONS

Markers (m); eight 1" (2.5 cm) buttons; tapestry needle.

GAUGE

16 sts and 24 rows = 4" (10 cm) in St st on middle-size needles.

17 sts and 26 rows = 4" (10 cm) in stem patt on middle-size needles.

Stitch Guide

seed stitch
(multiple of 2 sts)

ROW 1: (RS) *K1, p1; rep from * to end.

ROW 2: *P1, k1; rep from * to end.

Rep Rows 1 and 2 for patt.

seed stitch
(multiple of 2 sts + 1)

ROW 1: *K1, p1; rep from * to last st, k1.

Rep Row 1 for patt.

stem

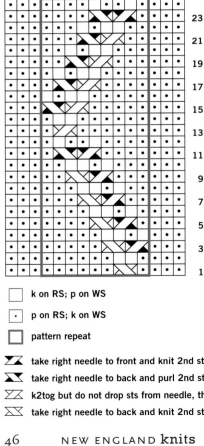

☐ k on RS; p on WS

· p on RS; k on WS

☐ pattern repeat

take right needle to front and knit 2nd st, then purl first st; drop both sts from needle

take right needle to back and purl 2nd st tbl, then knit first st; drop both sts from needle

k2tog but do not drop sts from needle, then knit first st again; drop both sts from needle

take right needle to back and knit 2nd st tbl, then knit both sts tog tbl; drop both sts from needle

Top

Right Sleeve

With middle-size needles, CO 38 (42, 46, 50, 54) sts.

Work in seed st (see Stitch Guide) for 1" (2.5 cm), ending with a WS row. Change to St st.

NEXT ROW: (RS; inc row) K1, RLI (see Glossary), knit to last st, LLI (see Glossary), k1—2 sts inc'd.

Rep inc row every 4th row 0 (0, 0, 0, 3) more times, every 6th row 7 (7, 11, 15, 13) times, then every 8th row 6 (6, 3, 0, 0) times—66 (70, 76, 82, 88) sts.

Work even until piece measures 19" (48.5 cm) from CO, ending with a WS row. *Note:* Count rows after last inc row so that left sleeve can be worked to match.

Cast On for Body Top

Using the cable method (see Glossary), CO 5 sts at beg of next 2 rows—76 (80, 86, 92, 98) sts. Work even until piece measures 4 (5, 6, 7, 8)" (10 [12.5, 15, 18, 20.5] cm) from CO for body, ending with a WS row.

Divide for Neck

NEXT ROW: (RS) K37 (39, 42, 45, 48), attach a new strand of yarn, BO 2 sts, knit to end—37 (39, 42, 45, 48) sts rem for each of front and back.

Working front and back at the same time, work even until piece measures 4" (10 cm) from neck division, ending with a WS row.

Finish Right Front

NEXT ROW: BO 37 (39, 42, 45, 48) front sts—37 (39, 42, 45, 48) sts rem for back.

Work even for 1" (2.5 cm), ending with a WS row.

Begin Left Front

NEXT ROW: With a new strand of yarn and using the long-tail method (see Glossary), CO 37 (39, 42, 45, 48) sts for front. (Do not join front to back.)

Working front and back separately at the same time, work even for 4" (10 cm), ending with a WS row—back neck measures about 9" (23 cm).

Join Back and Front

NEXT ROW: (RS) K37 (39, 42, 45, 48) front sts; with same strand of yarn, CO 2 sts, k37 (39, 42, 45, 48) back sts—76 (80, 86, 92, 98) sts total. Cut other strand of yarn.

Work even until piece measures 4 (5, 6, 7, 8)" (10 [12.5, 15, 18, 20.5] cm) from join, ending with a RS row.

Left Sleeve

BO 5 sts at beg of next 2 rows—66 (70, 76, 82, 88) sts rem.

Work the same number of rows as there are between last right sleeve inc and CO for body top, ending with a WS row.

NEXT ROW: (RS; dec row) K1, ssk, knit to last 3 sts, k2tog, k1—2 sts dec'd.

REP DEC row every 8th row 6 (6, 3, 0, 0) more times, every 6th row 7 (7, 11, 15, 13) times, then every 4th row 0 (0, 0, 0, 3) times—38 (42, 46, 50, 54) sts rem; sleeve measures 18" (45.5 cm) from body BO.

Work even in seed st for 1" (2.5 cm), ending with a WS row. BO all sts loosely.

Bottom

With middle-size needles, CO 177 (195, 213, 231, 249) sts.

Work in seed st until piece measures 1" (2.5 cm) from CO, ending with a WS row.

Work Rows 1–24 of Stem chart once, then work Rows 1–5 once more.

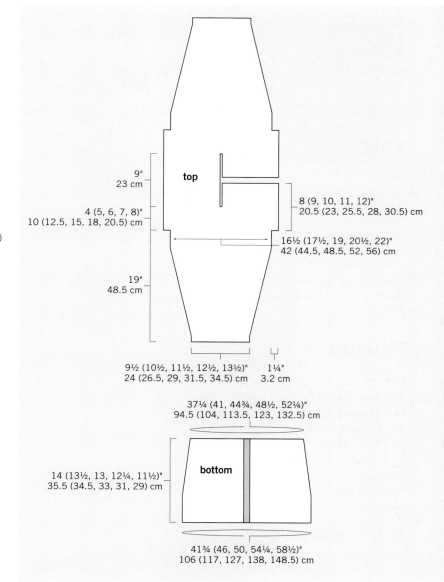

whale watch
HAT

DESIGNER
Kate Gagnon Osborn

This quirky beret was inspired by Kate's love for all things New England, such as the outrageous whale-embroidered khakis worn by Vineyard vacationers and the enduring combination of navy and white. The whimsical colorwork gives a classic whale motif a modern twist, and colorful chevrons grace the base and the crown of this beret.

finished size
18" (45.5 cm) brim circumference, 27½" (70 cm) circumference at widest point, and 7¾" (19.5 cm) tall.

YARN
Fingering (Super Fine #1).

shown here: The Fibre Company Canopy Fingering (50% baby alpaca, 30% merino, 20% bamboo; 200 yd [183 m]/50 g): orchid (white; MC), macaw (navy; CC1), blue quandons (light blue; CC2), and fern (light green; CC3), 1 skein each.

NEEDLES
U.S. size 0 (2 mm): 16" (40 cm) circular (cir). U.S. size 2 (2.75 mm): 20" (50 cm) cir and set of 4 or 5 double-pointed (dpn). Adjust needle size if necessary to obtain the correct gauge.

NOTIONS
Marker (m); tapestry needle.

GAUGE
28 sts and 32 rows = 4" (10 cm) in whale patt on larger needle.

51

Hat

With smaller needle and MC, CO 144 sts. Break yarn.

With CC1, knit 1 row.

Place marker (pm) and join for working in the rnd, being careful not to twist sts.

Work in k1, p1 rib for 1" (2.5 cm).

NEXT RND: (inc rnd) *K2, k1f&b; rep from * to end—192 sts.

Change to larger cir needle. Work Rows 1–58 of Whale chart—32 sts rem.

Use CC1 for remainder of hat.

NEXT RND: Knit.

NEXT RND: (dec rnd) *K1, sl 2 as if to k2tog, k1, p2sso; rep from * to end—16 sts rem.

NEXT RND: (dec rnd) *K2tog; rep from * to end—8 sts rem.

Break yarn, leaving an 8" (20.5 cm) tail. Thread through rem sts, pull tight to gather, and fasten off on WS.

Finishing

Weave in loose ends. Block to measurements.

whale

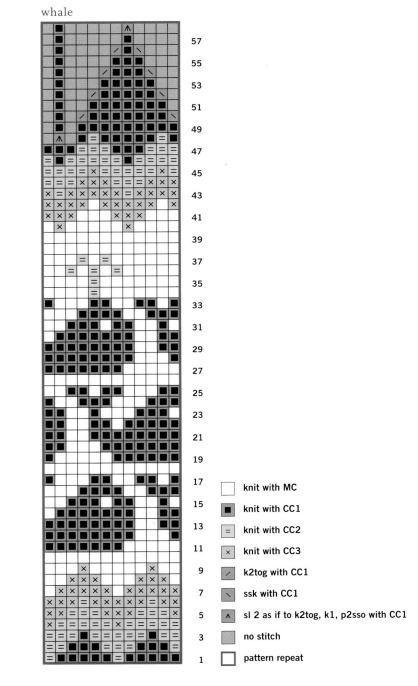

knit with MC

knit with CC1

knit with CC2

knit with CC3

k2tog with CC1

ssk with CC1

sl 2 as if to k2tog, k1, p2sso with CC1

no stitch

pattern repeat

Catching Floats in Stranded Knitting

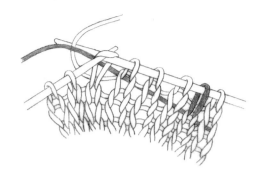

When one color in a stranded-colorwork pattern is used for four or more consecutive stitches, it creates a long float of the nonworking yarn across the back. Catching these floats as you work can help keep the tension even throughout your knitting and prevent the floats from being snagged on the wrong side.

To catch a float, work a few stitches of a long color repeat, then lift the nonworking yarn under or over the color you are currently working with. This traps the yarn and helps carry it to the point where you'll need to pick it up. Repeat every few stitches as needed, making sure you always catch the yarn in the same direction (either under or over).

fall
ON THE FARM

Working farms can still be found scattered throughout New England, some raising livestock, others growing produce. Apple and pumpkin picking are favorite autumn activities for natives and visitors alike. Although you may not want to wear these garments while doing actual farmwork, they are perfect for lighter outdoor chores. These pieces are warm, cozy, and easy to wear. Buttons and interesting stitch patterns add charming elements to classic shapes. Included in this section are a basketweave cable-trimmed hoodie, a peacoat-inspired sweater with a subtle knit and purl design on the back, and a pair of mittens with wonderfully simple colorwork. The knits in Fall on the Farm are ones that you will wear over and over.

brattleboro
HAT

DESIGNER
Melissa LaBarre

This hat is knitted in two directions: a ribbed band is worked from side to side to create the brim, and stitches are picked up along one side for the moss stitch crown. A button tab at the side gives this simple design a twist.

finished size
20" (51 cm) circumference at band.

YARN
Worsted (Medium #4).

shown here: Malabrigo Merino Worsted (100% wool; 215 yd [197 m]/100 g): #117 verde adriana, 1 skein.

NEEDLES
U.S. size 8 (5 mm): 16" (40 cm) circular (cir) and set of 4 or 5 double-pointed (dpn). Adjust needle size if necessary to obtain the correct gauge.

NOTIONS
Markers (m); two 1" (2.5 cm) buttons; tapestry needle.

GAUGE
18 sts and 25 rnds = 4" (10 cm) in moss st.

22 sts and 25 rows = 4" (10 cm) in k2, p2 rib, relaxed.

Hat

Ribbed Band

With cir needle, CO 20 sts. Do not join.

ROW 1: (RS) K3, *p2, k2; rep from * to last 5 sts, p2, k3.

ROW 2: Work sts as they appear.

Rep Rows 1 and 2 until piece measures 20" (51 cm) from CO, ending with a WS row. BO all sts in patt. Block piece to relax rib.

Body

With cir needle and RS facing, pick up and knit (see Glossary) 80 sts evenly spaced along one long edge of ribbed band. Place marker (pm) and join for working in the rnd.

Work Rnds 1–4 of moss st (see Stitch Guide) 3 times, then work Rnds 1–3 once more—15 rnds total.

NEXT RND: Cont in patt, *work 20 sts, pm; rep from * 3 more times.

Shape Crown

NEXT RND: (dec rnd) *K2tog, work in patt to 2 sts before m, ssk; rep from * 3 more times—8 sts dec'd.

Rep dec rnd every other rnd 7 more times, maintaining patt between m—16 sts rem.

Work 1 rnd even.

NEXT RND: (dec rnd) *K2tog, ssk; rep from * 3 more times—8 sts rem.

NEXT RND: [P1, k1] 4 times.

NEXT RND: (dec rnd) [K2tog] 4 times—4 sts rem.

Break yarn and draw through rem sts. Pull tight to gather and fasten off on WS.

Finishing

Buttonband

Pick up and knit 18 sts along one short edge of ribbed band.

ROW 1: (WS) *P2, k2; rep from * to last 2 sts, p2.

Work 2 more rows even in rib.

NEXT ROW: (RS; buttonhole row) K2, p1, p2tog, yo, k1, p2, k2, p2, k1, yo, p2tog, p1, k2.

NEXT ROW: *P2, k2; rep from * to last 2 sts, p2.

NEXT ROW: (RS; dec row) K2, p2tog, k2, p2, k2, p2, k2, p2tog, k2—16 sts rem.

NEXT ROW: P2, k1, p2, k2, p2, k2, p2, k1, p2.

NEXT ROW: (RS; dec row) K2, p2tog, k1, p2, k2, p2, k1, p2tog, k2—14 sts rem.

NEXT ROW: (WS; dec row) P2, k1, p1, k2tog, p2, k2tog, p1, k1, p2—12 sts rem.

With RS facing, BO all sts in patt. Weave in loose ends. Sew buttons to ribbed band opposite buttonholes.

Picking Up Stitches Evenly Along an Edge

When a pattern instructs you to pick up a specific number of
stitches along an edge, save yourself some frustration with a
simple trick. First, measure your piece, then gather locking
stitch markers or safety pins. If you have only a small area, you
may find that just dividing your piece into two sections will be
enough. For longer edges, use more markers and divide your
piece into four or more equal sections, using a ruler and placing
locking markers at even intervals along the piece. Now divide the
number of stitches that you need to pick up by the number of
sections you've created and you'll have a much more manageable
number to keep track of.

greenfield
CARDIGAN

DESIGNER
Melissa LaBarre

This garter-stitch cardigan is simple to knit, but the thoughtful details create an elegant sweater. The top-down raglan construction uses eyelet increases to accent the shaping, and a leaf detail at each front keeps it interesting. Three-quarter-length sleeves make it perfect for transitional weather.

finished size

36 (40, 44, 48, 52)" (91.5 [101.5, 112, 122, 132] cm) bust circumference, buttoned; cardigan shown measures 36" (91.5 cm).

YARN

DK (Light #3).

shown here: Shibui Merino Kid (55% kid mohair, 45% merino; 218 yd [199 m]/100 g): #MK7495 wasabi (yellow-green), 4 (5, 6, 7, 8) skeins.

NEEDLES

U.S. size 6 (4 mm): 32" (80 cm) circular (cir) and set of 4 or 5 double-pointed (dpn). Adjust needle size if necessary to obtain the correct gauge.

NOTIONS

6 markers (m); stitch holders or waste yarn; three ⅞" (2.2 cm) buttons; tapestry needle.

GAUGE

20 sts and 32 rows = 4" (10 cm) in garter st.

Cardigan

Neck

With cir needle and using the long-tail method (see Glossary), CO 118 sts. Do not join.

Knit 2 rows.

Shape Back Neck

Note: Do not pick up wraps from short-rows.

SHORT-ROW 1: (RS) K95, wrap next st, turn (see Glossary).

SHORT-ROW 2: (WS) K72, wrap next st, turn.

NEXT ROW: Knit to end.

NEXT ROW: Knit.

NEXT ROW: (RS; beg buttonhole row) K23, place marker (pm), k14, pm, k44, pm, k14, pm, k18, BO 2 sts, knit to end.

NEXT ROW: (WS; end buttonhole row) K3, use the backward-loop method (see Glossary) to CO 2 sts, knit to end of row.

Shape Raglan

ROW 1: (RS) [Knit to 1 st before m, yo, k1, sl m, k1, yo] 4 times, knit to end of row—8 sts inc'd.

leaf

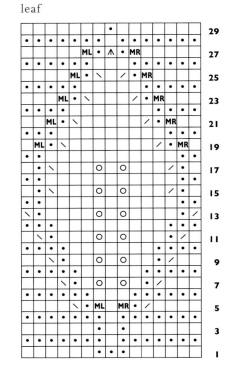

□	k on RS; p on WS
·	p on RS; k on WS
o	yo
╱	k2tog
╲	ssk
⋀	sl 2 as if to k2tog, k1, p2sso
MR	M I R
ML	M I L

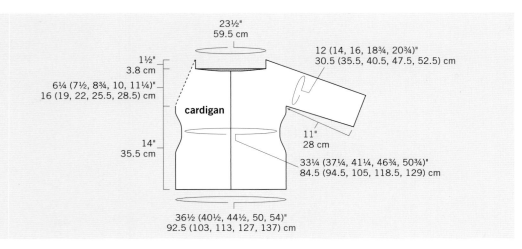

23½"
59.5 cm

1½"
3.8 cm

6¼ (7½, 8¾, 10, 11¼)"
16 (19, 22, 25.5, 28.5) cm

cardigan

12 (14, 16, 18¾, 20¾)"
30.5 (35.5, 40.5, 47.5, 52.5) cm

11"
28 cm

14"
35.5 cm

33¼ (37¼, 41¼, 46¾, 50¾)"
84.5 (94.5, 105, 118.5, 129) cm

36½ (40½, 44½, 50, 54)"
92.5 (103, 113, 127, 137) cm

ROW 2: [Knit to 1 st before m, p1, sl m, p1] 4 times, knit to end.

Rep last 2 rows 20 (25, 30, 35, 40) more times, and *at the same time* work buttonhole as before every 20th row 2 more times—286 (326, 366, 406, 446) sts.

Divide for Body and Sleeves

NEXT ROW: (RS) Knit to first m, remove m, place 56 (66, 76, 86, 96) sleeve sts onto holder, remove m, use the backward-loop method to CO 2 (2, 2, 4, 4) sts for underarm, pm, CO 2 (2, 2, 4, 4) sts for underarm, knit to next m, remove m, place 56 (66, 76, 86, 96) sleeve sts onto holder, remove m, use the backward-loop method to CO 2 (2, 2, 4, 4) sts for underarm, pm, CO 2 (2, 2, 4, 4) sts for underarm, knit to end—182 (202, 222, 250, 270) sts rem for body.

Knit 9 rows.

Shape Waist

NEXT ROW: (RS; dec row) *Knit to 6 sts before m, ssk, k4, sl m, k4, k2tog; rep from * once more, knit to end—4 sts dec'd.

Rep dec row every 8th row 3 more times—166 (186, 206, 234, 254) sts rem.

Work 7 rows even.

NEXT ROW: (RS; inc row) *Knit to 5 sts before m, k1f&b (see Glossary), k4, sl m, k4, k1f&b; rep from * once more, knit to end—4 sts inc'd.

Rep inc row every 8th row 3 more times—182 (202, 222, 250, 270) sts.

Leaf Motif

Work even until piece measures 10" (25.5 cm) from underarm, ending with a WS row.

NEXT ROW: (RS) K10, pm, work Row 1 of Leaf chart, pm, knit to last 25 sts, pm, work Row 1 of Leaf chart, pm, k10.

Cont in patt through Row 29 of chart.

Cont in garter st until piece measures 14" (35.5 cm) from underarm, ending with a RS row. With WS facing, BO all sts kwise.

Sleeves

Place 56 (66, 76, 86, 96) held sleeve sts onto dpn. Beg at center of underarm, pick up and knit (see Glossary) 2 (2, 2, 4, 4) sts in CO sts, k56 (66, 76, 86, 96), pick up and knit 2 (2, 2, 4, 4) sts in CO sts, pm and join for working in the rnd—60 (70, 80, 94, 104) sts. Work in garter st (knit 1 rnd, purl 1 rnd) until piece measures 11" (28 cm) from underarm, ending with a purl rnd.

BO all sts kwise.

Finishing

With RS facing, pick up and knit 79 (83, 88, 93, 98) sts along center front edge of right front. Knit 2 rows. With WS facing, BO all sts kwise. Rep for left front. Sew buttons to left front opposite buttonholes.

Weave in loose ends. Block to measurements.

portland
MITTENS

DESIGNER
Carrie Bostick Hoge

These mittens combine color and texture in a honeycomb pattern. The three-dimensional stitch pattern keeps your hands especially warm by trapping additional air, and the snug ribbed cuffs keep the breezes out. Worked mostly in muted tones, the mittens have a splash of color in contrasting-color thumbs and striped cuffs.

finished size
8" (20.5 cm) hand circumference and 10" (25.5 cm) long.

YARN
Worsted (Medium #4).

shown here: Reynolds Lite Lopi (100% virgin wool; 109 yd [100 m]/50 g): #054 light gray (A), #1402 blue (B), and #0008 light denim heather (C), 1 skein each.

NEEDLES
U.S. sizes 7 and 8 (4.5 and 5 mm): set of 4 or 5 double-pointed (dpn). Adjust needle size if necessary to obtain the correct gauge.

NOTIONS
Waste yarn in same weight as main yarn; tapestry needle.

GAUGE
24 sts and 41 rows = 4" (10 cm) in slip st patt on larger needles.

Stitch Guide

slip-stitch pattern
(multiple of 6 sts)

RNDS 1–4: With C, *sl 2, k4; rep from * to end.

RNDS 5 AND 6: With A, purl.

RNDS 7–10: With C, k3, sl 2, *k4, sl 2; rep from * to last st, k1.

RNDS 11 AND 12: With A, purl.

Rep Rnds 1–12 for patt.

Mitten

With smaller needles and A, CO 48 sts. Divide sts onto dpn and join for working in the rnd, being careful not to twist sts. Work in k2, p2 rib for 8 rnds.

Maintaining k2, p2 rib, work color stripes as foll: 2 rnds with B; 4 rnds with A; 2 rnds with B; 6 rnds with A. Change to larger needles. Purl 1 rnd.

Work Rnds 1–12 of slip st patt (see Stitch Guide) once, then work Rnds 1–5 once more.

Place Thumb

NEXT RND: With waste yarn, p10; sl these 10 sts to left needle. Work Rnd 6 of patt across all sts.

Cont in patt until piece measures 9" (23 cm) from CO, ending with Rnd 12 of patt.

Shape Top

RND 1: (dec rnd) With C, *sl 2, k2, k2tog; rep from * to end—40 sts rem.

RNDS 2 AND 3: *Sl 2, k3; rep from * to end.

RND 4: (dec rnd) *Sl 2, k1, k2tog; rep from * to end—32 sts rem.

RNDS 5, 7, AND 9: With A, purl.

RND 6: (dec rnd) *P2, p2tog; rep from * to end—24 sts rem.

RND 8: (dec rnd) *P1, p2tog; rep from * to end—16 sts rem.

RND 10: (dec rnd) *P2tog; rep from * to end—8 sts rem.

Break yarn, leaving a 6" (15 cm) tail. Draw tail through rem sts, pull tight to gather, and fasten off on WS.

Thumb

Carefully remove waste yarn and place revealed sts onto larger needles—20 sts total; 10 sts each from lower and upper edges. Attach yarn B. K10 lower sts, pick up and knit (see Glossary) 1 st in space between lower and upper sets of sts, k10 upper sts, pick up and knit 1 st in space between upper and lower sts—22 sts total. Join for working in the rnd.

NEXT RND: (dec rnd) *K9, k2tog; rep from * once more—20 sts rem.

Work even in St st until thumb measures 1½" (3.8 cm), or 1" (2.5 cm) less than desired finished length.

Shape Thumb

RND 1: (dec rnd) *K5, k2tog; rep from * once more, k4, k2tog—17 sts rem.

RNDS 2, 4, 6, AND 8: Knit.

RND 3: (dec rnd) *K4, k2tog; rep from * once more, k3, k2tog—14 sts rem.

RND 5: (dec rnd) *K3, k2tog; rep from * once more, k2, k2tog—11 sts rem.

RND 7: (dec rnd) *K2, k2tog; rep from * once more, k1, k2tog—8 sts rem.

RND 9: (dec rnd) *K1, k2tog; rep from * once more, k2tog—5 sts rem.

Break yarn, leaving a 6" (15 cm) tail. Draw tail through rem sts, pull tight to gather, and fasten off on WS.

Finishing

Weave in loose ends.

melrose PEACOAT

DESIGNER
Cecily Glowik MacDonald

This cropped peacoat-style sweater has a classic double-breasted shape with a modern length. Covered buttons evoke the details on the traditional peacoat, but sew-on snaps concealed beneath the front panel keep the lines crisp. A rose pattern worked on the upper back adds an interesting and slightly feminine detail.

finished size

39 (42½, 46, 50, 53½)" (99 [108, 117, 127, 136] cm) bust circumference, closed; coat shown measures 39" (99 cm).

YARN

Chunky (Bulky #5).

shown here: Brown Sheep Lamb's Pride Bulky (85% wool, 15% mohair; 125 yd [114 m]/113 g): #M145 spice, 8 (9, 9, 10, 11) skeins.

NEEDLES

U.S. size 10 (6 mm). Adjust needle size if necessary to obtain the correct gauge.

NOTIONS

Markers (m); six ⅞" (2.2 cm) buttons; three size 4 sew-on snaps; matching thread and sewing needle; tapestry needle.

GAUGE

13 sts and 19 rows = 4" (10 cm) in St st.

Stitch Guide

seed stitch
(multiple of 2 sts + 1)

ROW 1: *K1, p1; rep from * to last st, k1.

Rep Row 1 for patt.

seed stitch
(multiple of 2 sts)

ROW 1: (RS) *K1, p1; rep from * to end.

ROW 2: *P1, k1; rep from * to end.

Rep Rows 1 and 2 for patt.

Back

CO 63 (69, 75, 81, 87) sts. Work in seed st (see Stitch Guide) until piece measures 2" (5 cm) from CO, ending with a WS row. Change to St st and work even until piece measures 11" (28 cm) from CO, ending with a WS row.

NEXT ROW: K14 (17, 20, 23, 26), place marker (pm), work 35 sts according to Flower Panel chart, pm, knit to end.

Cont in patt, working sts at beg and end of needle in St st and sts between markers according to Flower Panel chart, until chart is complete. *At the same time*, when piece measures 14 (13½, 13, 12½, 12)" (35.5 [34.5, 33, 31.5, 30.5] cm) from CO, ending with a WS row, shape armholes as foll.

Shape Armholes

BO 4 (4, 5, 5, 5) sts at beg of next 2 rows—55 (61, 65, 71, 77) sts rem.

NEXT ROW: (RS; dec row) Ssk, work in patt to last 2 sts, k2tog—2 sts dec'd.

Rep dec row every RS row 3 (4, 4, 4, 4) more times—47 (51, 55, 61, 67) sts rem. When Flower Panel chart is complete, remove m and work all sts in St st. Work even until armholes measure 8 (8½, 9, 9½, 10)" (20.5 [21.5, 23, 24, 25.5] cm), ending with a WS row.

flower panel

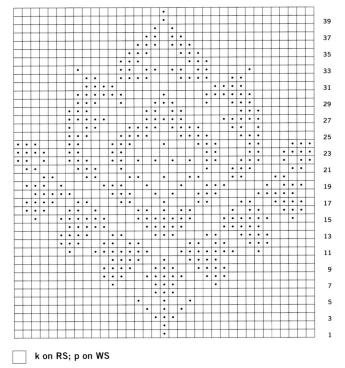

39
37
35
33
31
29
27
25
23
21
19
17
15
13
11
9
7
5
3
1

☐ **k on RS; p on WS**

· **p on RS; k on WS**

Shape Shoulders

BO 6 (6, 7, 8, 9) sts at beg of next 2 rows, then BO 6 (7, 8, 8, 9) sts at beg of foll 2 rows—23 (25, 25, 29, 31) sts rem. BO all sts.

Right Front

CO 41 (44, 47, 50, 53) sts. Work in seed st until piece measures 2" (5 cm) from CO, ending with a WS row.

NEXT ROW: (RS) Work 17 sts in seed st, pm, work in St st to end.

Cont in patt as established until piece measures 14 (13½, 13, 12½, 12)" (35.5 [34.5, 33, 31.5, 30.5] cm) from CO, ending with a RS row.

Shape Armhole

BO 4 (4, 5, 5, 5) sts at beg of next row—37 (40, 42, 45, 48) sts rem.

NEXT ROW: (RS; dec row) Work to last 3 sts, k2tog, k1—1 st dec'd.

Rep dec row every RS row 3 (4, 4, 4, 4) more times—33 (35, 37, 40, 43) sts rem. Work even until armhole measures 6 (6½, 7, 7½, 8)" (15 [16.5, 18, 19, 20.5] cm), ending with a WS row.

Shape Neck

BO 19 (19, 19, 21, 22) sts at beg of next row—14 (16, 18, 19, 21) sts rem. Work 1 WS row even.

NEXT ROW: (RS; dec row) K1, ssk, knit to end—1 st dec'd.

Rep dec row every RS row 1 (2, 2, 2, 2) more time(s)—12 (13, 15, 16, 18) sts rem. Work even until armhole measures 8 (8½, 9, 9½, 10)" (20.5 [21.5, 23, 24, 25.5] cm), ending with a RS row.

Shape Shoulder

BO 6 (6, 7, 8, 9) sts at beg of next row—6 (7, 8, 8, 9) sts rem. Work 1 RS row even. BO all sts.

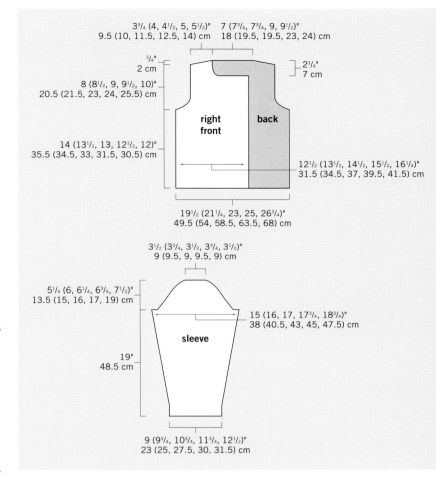

Left Front

CO 31 (34, 37, 40, 43) sts. Work in seed st until piece measures 2" (5 cm) from CO, ending with a WS row.

NEXT ROW: (RS) Work 24 (27, 30, 33, 36) sts in St st, pm, work in seed st to end.

Cont in patt as established until piece measures 14 (13½, 13, 12½, 12)" (35.5 [34.5, 33, 31.5, 30.5] cm) from CO, ending with a WS row.

Shape Armhole

BO 4 (4, 5, 5, 5) sts at beg of next row—27 (30, 32, 35, 38) sts rem. Work 1 WS row even.

NEXT ROW: (RS; dec row) K1, ssk, work to end—1 st dec'd.

Rep dec row every RS row 3 (4, 4, 4, 4) more times—23 (25, 27, 30, 33) sts rem. Work even until armhole measures 6 (6½, 7, 7½, 8)" (15 [16.5, 18, 19, 20.5] cm), ending with a RS row.

Shape Neck

BO 9 (9, 9, 11, 12) sts at beg of next row—14 (16, 18, 19, 21) sts rem.

NEXT ROW: (RS; dec row) Work to last 3 sts, k2tog, k1—1 st dec'd.

Rep dec row every RS row 1 (2, 2, 2, 2) more time(s)—12 (13, 15, 16, 18) sts rem. Work even until armhole measures 8 (8½, 9, 9½, 10)" (20.5 [21.5, 23, 24, 25.5] cm), ending with a WS row.

Shape Shoulder

BO 6 (6, 7, 8, 9) sts at beg of next RS row—6 (7, 8, 8, 9) sts rem. Work 1 WS row even. BO all sts.

Sleeves

CO 29 (32, 35, 38, 41) sts. Work in seed st until piece measures 2" (5 cm) from CO, ending with a WS row.

Shape Sleeve

Change to St st.

NEXT ROW: (RS; inc row) K1, M1L (see Glossary), knit to last st, M1R (see Glossary), k1—2 sts inc'd.

Rep inc row every 8th row 5 more times, then every 10th row 4 times—49 (52, 55, 58, 61) sts. If necessary, work even until piece measures 19" (48.5 cm) from CO, ending with a WS row.

Shape Cap

BO 4 (4, 5, 5, 5) sts at beg of next 2 rows—41 (44, 45, 48, 51) sts rem.

NEXT ROW: (RS; dec row) K1, ssk, knit to last 3 sts, k2tog, k1—2 sts dec'd.

Rep dec row every RS row 8 (10, 11, 12, 14) more times—23 (22, 21, 22, 21) sts rem.

NEXT ROW: (WS; dec row) P1, p2tog, purl to last 3 sts, ssp (see Glossary), p1—2 sts dec'd.

Dec 1 st each end of needle as established every row 3 (2, 2, 2, 2) more times—15 (16, 15, 16, 15) sts rem. BO 2 sts at beg of next 2 rows—11 (12, 11, 12, 11) sts rem. BO all sts.

Finishing

Sew shoulder seams. Sew in sleeves. Sew sleeve and side seams, turning up cuff and sewing seam on opposite side of sleeve.

Collar

With RS facing and beg at right front neck edge, pick up and knit (see Glossary) 68 (74, 74, 80, 84) sts evenly spaced around neck. Work even in seed st until piece measures 1½" (3.8 cm) from pick-up row, ending with a RS row. With WS facing, BO all sts kwise. Weave in loose ends.

With sewing needle and thread, sew 1 snap bottom to left front collar 2 rows down from top and 2 sts in from edge. Sew second snap 4" (10 cm) below first, and sew third snap 3½" (9 cm) below second. Sew snap tops to WS of right front opposite snap bottoms. Sew 2 buttons to RS of right front collar above seed-stitch panel, each ½" (1.3 cm) from side of panel. Sew 2 more buttons 3¾" (9.5 cm) below first buttons, then sew last 2 buttons 3¾" (9.5 cm) below those.

augusta
CARDIGAN

DESIGNER
Cecily Glowik MacDonald

You'll reach for this comfortable cardigan again and again, from the first chill of fall through the last cool days of spring. With a classic cable pattern and worked in soft, earthy yarn, this cabled cardigan is perfect for a man or a woman; waist shaping is omitted to flatter a variety of figures.

finished size

32 (36, 40, 44, 48, 52, 56)" (81.5 [91.5, 101.5, 112, 122, 132, 142] cm) chest/bust circumference; cardigan shown measures 40" (101.5 cm).

YARN

Worsted (Medium #4).

shown here: Classic Elite Montera Heathers (50% wool, 50% llama; 127 yd [116 m]/100 g): #3844 bronze medal (gray-green), 7 (8, 8, 9, 10, 11, 11) hanks.

NEEDLES

U.S. size 8 (5 mm): 24" (60 cm) circular (cir). Adjust needle size if necessary to obtain the correct gauge.

NOTIONS

Markers (m); cable needle (cn); six 1" (2.5 cm) buttons; tapestry needle.

GAUGE

16 sts and 22 rows = 4" (10 cm) in St st.

12 sts of Cable chart = 2" (5 cm) wide.

Back

CO 64 (72, 80, 88, 96, 104, 112) sts. Do not join.

Begin rib patt as foll:

NEXT ROW: (WS) P2, k4, *p4, k4; rep from * to last 2 sts, p2.

NEXT ROW: (RS) Work sts as they appear.

Work in patt as established until piece measures 1" (2.5 cm) from CO, ending with a WS row.

Change to St st and work even until piece measures 16½ (16, 15½, 15, 14½, 14, 13½)" (42 [40.5, 39.5, 38, 37, 35.5, 34.5] cm) from CO, ending with a WS row.

Shape Armholes

BO 4 (4, 5, 5, 5, 6, 6) sts at beg of next 2 rows—56 (64, 70, 78, 86, 92, 100) sts rem.

NEXT ROW: (RS; dec row) K1, ssk, knit to last 3 sts, k2tog, k1—2 sts dec'd.

Rep dec row every RS row 3 (3, 3, 4, 4, 4, 4) more times—48 (56, 62, 68, 76, 82, 90) sts rem.

Work even until armholes measure 8½ (9, 9½, 10, 10½, 11, 11½)" (21.5 [23, 24, 25.5, 26.5, 28, 29] cm), ending with a WS row.

Shape Shoulders

BO 5 (7, 8, 9, 10, 11, 13) sts at beg of next 2 rows—38 (42, 46, 50, 56, 60, 64) sts rem. BO 5 (7, 8, 9, 11, 12, 13) sts at beg of next 2 rows— 28 (28, 30, 32, 34, 36, 38) sts rem. BO all sts.

Left Front

CO 37 (45, 49, 53, 61, 65, 69) sts. Do not join.

SET-UP ROW: (WS) Work 2 (1, 3, 5, 1, 2, 3) sts in St st, [work Cable chart, work 4 sts in St st] 2 (2, 2, 3, 3, 3, 4) times, [work Cable chart] 0 (1, 1, 0, 1, 1, 0) time, work 0 (0, 2, 0, 0, 3, 0) sts in St st, work 3 (0, 0, 0, 0, 0, 2) sts in rev St st.

cable

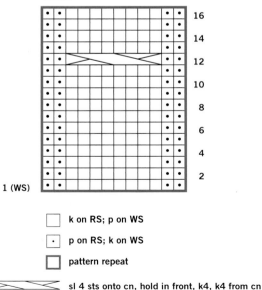

□ k on RS; p on WS

· p on RS; k on WS

□ pattern repeat

⋈ sl 4 sts onto cn, hold in front, k4, k4 from cn

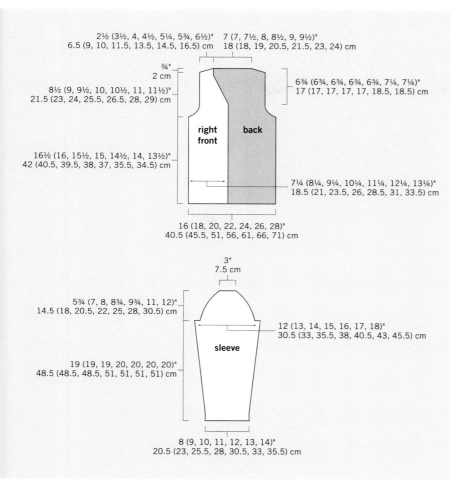

2½ (3½, 4, 4½, 5¼, 5¾, 6½)"
6.5 (9, 10, 11.5, 13.5, 14.5, 16.5) cm

7 (7, 7½, 8, 8½, 9, 9½)"
18 (18, 19, 20.5, 21.5, 23, 24) cm

¾"
2 cm

8½ (9, 9½, 10, 10½, 11, 11½)"
21.5 (23, 24, 25.5, 26.5, 28, 29) cm

6¾ (6¾, 6¾, 6¾, 6¾, 7¼, 7¼)"
17 (17, 17, 17, 17, 18.5, 18.5) cm

right front

back

16½ (16, 15½, 15, 14½, 14, 13½)"
42 (40.5, 39.5, 38, 37, 35.5, 34.5) cm

7¼ (8¼, 9¼, 10¼, 11¼, 12¼, 13¼)"
18.5 (21, 23.5, 26, 28.5, 31, 33.5) cm

16 (18, 20, 22, 24, 26, 28)"
40.5 (45.5, 51, 56, 61, 66, 71) cm

3"
7.5 cm

5¾ (7, 8, 8¾, 9¾, 11, 12)"
14.5 (18, 20.5, 22, 25, 28, 30.5) cm

12 (13, 14, 15, 16, 17, 18)"
30.5 (33, 35.5, 38, 40.5, 43, 45.5) cm

sleeve

19 (19, 19, 20, 20, 20, 20)"
48.5 (48.5, 48.5, 51, 51, 51, 51) cm

8 (9, 10, 11, 12, 13, 14)"
20.5 (23, 25.5, 28, 30.5, 33, 35.5) cm

Work in patt as established until piece measures 16½ (16, 15½, 15, 14½, 14, 13½)" (42 [40.5, 39.5, 38, 37, 35.5, 34.5] cm) from CO, ending with a WS row.

Shape Armhole

Note: Neck shaping beg before armhole shaping ends; read the foll sections all the way through before proceeding.

BO 4 (4, 5, 5, 5, 6, 6) sts at beg of next row—33 (41, 44, 48, 56, 59, 63) sts rem. Work 1 WS row even in patt.

NEXT ROW: (RS; dec row) K1, ssk or ssp (see Glossary) as needed to maintain patt, work in patt to end—1 st dec'd.

Rep dec row every RS row 2 (6, 6, 7, 11, 11, 11) more times—3 (7, 7, 8, 12, 12, 12) sts dec'd for armhole.

Shape Neck

At the same time, when armhole measures 2½ (3, 3½, 4, 4½, 4½, 5)" (6.5 [7.5, 9, 10, 11.5, 11.5, 12.5] cm), ending with a WS row, shape neck as foll:

NEXT ROW: (RS; dec row) Work to last 3 sts, k2tog or p2tog as needed to maintain patt, k1—1 st dec'd.

NEXT ROW: (WS; dec row) P1, k2tog or p2tog as needed to maintain patt, work to end—1 st dec'd.

Dec 1 st at neck edge as established every row 18 (18, 19, 20, 21, 22, 23) more times—10 (14, 16, 18, 21, 23, 26) sts rem after all shaping is complete.

Work even in patt until armhole measures 8½ (9, 9½, 10, 10½, 11, 11½)" (21.5 [23, 24, 25.5, 26.5, 28, 29] cm), ending with a WS row.

Shape Shoulder

BO 5 (7, 8, 9, 10, 11, 13) sts at beg of next row—5 (7, 8, 9, 11, 12, 13) sts rem. Work 1 WS row even. BO all sts.

Right Front

CO 37 (45, 49, 53, 61, 65, 69) sts. Do not join.

SET-UP ROW: (WS) Work 3 (0, 0, 0, 0, 0, 2) sts in rev St st, work 0 (0, 2, 0, 0, 3, 0) sts in St st, [work Cable chart] 0 (1, 1, 0, 1, 1, 0) time, [work 4 sts in St st, work Cable chart] 2 (2, 2, 3, 3, 3, 4) times, work 2 (1, 3, 5, 1, 2, 3) sts in St st.

Work in patt as established until piece measures 16½ (16, 15½, 15, 14½, 14, 13½)" (42 [40.5, 39.5, 38, 37, 35.5, 34.5] cm) from CO, ending with a RS row.

Shape Armhole

Note: Neck shaping beg before armhole shaping ends; read the foll sections all the way through before proceeding.

BO 4 (4, 5, 5, 5, 6, 6) sts at beg of next row—33 (41, 44, 48, 56, 59, 63) sts rem.

NEXT ROW: (RS; dec row) Work in patt to last 3 sts, k2tog or p2tog as needed to maintain patt, k1—1 st dec'd.

Rep dec row every RS row 2 (6, 6, 7, 11, 11, 11) more times—3 (7, 7, 8, 12, 12, 12) sts dec'd for armhole.

Shape Neck

At the same time, when armhole measures 2½ (3, 3½, 4, 4½, 4½, 5)" (6.5 [7.5, 9, 10, 11.5, 11.5, 12.5] cm), ending with a WS row, shape neck as foll:

NEXT ROW: (RS; dec row) K1, ssk or ssp as needed to maintain patt, work to end—1 st dec'd.

NEXT ROW: (WS; dec row) Work to last 3 sts, ssk or ssp as needed to maintain patt, p1—1 st dec'd.

Dec 1 st at neck edge as established every row 18 (18, 19, 20, 21, 22, 23) more times—10 (14, 16, 18, 21, 23, 26) sts rem after all shaping is complete.

Work even in patt until armhole measures 8½ (9, 9½, 10, 10½, 11, 11½)" (21.5 [23, 24, 25.5, 26.5, 28, 29] cm), ending with a RS row.

Shape Shoulder

BO 5 (7, 8, 9, 10, 11, 13) sts at beg of next row—5 (7, 8, 9, 11, 12, 13) sts rem. Work 1 RS row even. BO all sts.

Sleeves

CO 36 (40, 44, 48, 52, 56, 60) sts. Do not join.

NEXT ROW: (WS) K0 (2, 0, 0, 0, 2, 0), p4 (4, 0, 2, 4, 4, 0), [k4, p4] 1 (1, 2, 2, 2, 2, 3) time(s), place marker (pm), work Cable chart, pm, [p4, k4] 1 (1, 2, 2, 2, 2, 3) time(s), p4 (4, 0, 2, 4, 4, 0), k0 (2, 0, 0, 0, 2, 0).

NEXT ROW: (RS) Work sts as they appear to m, work Cable chart to next m, work sts as they appear to end.

Work in patt as established until piece measures 1" (2.5 cm) from CO, ending with a WS row.

NEXT ROW: Work in St st to m, work Cable chart to m, work in St st to end.

Rep last row until piece measures 1½" (3.8 cm) from CO, ending with a WS row.

Shape Sleeve

NEXT ROW: (RS; inc row) K1, RLI (see Glossary), work in patt to last st, LLI, k1—2 sts inc'd.

Rep inc row every 12th row 7 more times—52 (56, 60, 64, 68, 72, 76) sts. Work even until piece measures 19 (19, 19, 20, 20, 20, 20)" (48.5 [48.5, 48.5, 51, 51, 51, 51] cm) from CO, ending with a WS row.

Shape Cap

BO 4 (4, 5, 5, 5, 6, 6) sts at beg of next 2 rows—44 (48, 50, 54, 58, 60, 64) sts rem.

NEXT ROW: (RS; dec row) K1, ssk, work in patt to last 3 sts, k2tog, k1—2 sts dec'd.

Rep dec row every RS row 6 (5, 4, 6, 7, 6, 7) more times, every 4th row 2 (3, 5, 5, 6, 8, 9) times, then every RS row 3 (5, 5, 5, 5, 5, 5) times—20 sts rem. Work 1 WS row even. BO 4 sts at beg of next 2 rows—12 sts rem. BO rem sts as foll: BO 3 sts in patt, k2tog, pass 2nd st over k2tog to BO 1 st, BO 2 sts in patt, k2tog, pass 2nd st over k2tog to BO 1 st, BO last 3 sts in patt.

Finishing

Block pieces to measurements. Sew shoulder seams. Sew in sleeves. Sew sleeve and side seams.

Band

With RS facing and beg at bottom edge of right front, pick up and knit (see Glossary) 112 (112, 111, 114, 113, 112, 111) sts along right front edge, 28 (28, 30, 32, 34, 36, 38) sts along back neck, and 112 (112, 111, 114, 113, 112, 111) sts along left front edge—252 (252, 252, 260, 260, 260, 260) sts total. Do not join.

ROW 1: (WS) *P4, k4; rep from * to last 4 sts, p4.

ROW 2: Work sts as they appear.

ROW 3: (WS; buttonhole row) [P2, yo, p2tog, k4, p4, k4] 6 times, work in rib as established to end.

ROW 4: Work sts as they appear, working yo's as k1 through back loop (tbl).

ROW 5: Work sts as they appear.

BO all sts kwise. Sew buttons to right front band opposite buttonholes.

Weave in loose ends.

mystic PULLOVER

DESIGNER
Melissa LaBarre

This cowl-neck pullover has hidden charms—a pocket on each side seam is lined for extra warmth on cold days (and the contrasting color is a fun private detail). The fully fashioned waist shaping takes center stage beside the dramatic zigzag cable pattern.

finished size

34 (38, 42½, 46½, 50)" (86.5 [96.5, 108, 118, 127] cm) bust circumference; sweater shown measures 34" (86.5 cm).

YARN

Worsted (Medium #4).

shown here: The Fibre Company Organik (70% organic wool, 15% silk, 15% baby alpaca; 98 yd [90 m]/50 g): atoll (blue; MC), 12 (14, 16, 19, 20) skeins, and aquatic forest (aqua; CC), 1 skein.

NEEDLES

U.S. size 8 (5 mm): 24" (60 cm) circular (cir) and set of 4 or 5 double-pointed (dpn). Adjust needle size if necessary to obtain the correct gauge.

NOTIONS

Markers (m); cable needle (cn); tapestry needle.

GAUGE

17 sts and 27 rows = 4" (10 cm) in St st.

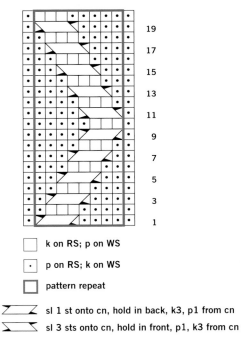

cable

		19
		17
		15
		13
		11
		9
		7
		5
		3
		1

☐ k on RS; p on WS

· p on RS; k on WS

☐ pattern repeat

⟋ sl 1 st onto cn, hold in back, k3, p1 from cn

⟍ sl 3 sts onto cn, hold in front, p1, k3 from cn

Back

With cir needle and MC, CO 80 (88, 98, 106, 114) sts. Do not join.

NEXT ROW: (RS) K23 (27, 32, 36, 40), place marker (pm), work 34 sts according to Row 1 of Cable chart, pm, knit to end.

Work in patt as established, working St st over beg and end of row and cable patt between m, until piece measures 5" (12.5 cm) from CO, ending with a WS row.

Shape Waist

NEXT ROW: (RS; dec row) Work to 2 sts before m, ssk, sl m, work in patt to m, sl m, k2tog, knit to end—2 sts dec'd.

Rep dec row every 8th row 2 more times—74 (82, 92, 100, 108) sts rem.

Work 7 rows even.

NEXT ROW: (RS; inc row) Knit to m, M1 (see Glossary), sl m, work in patt to m, sl m, M1, knit to end—2 sts inc'd.

Rep inc row every 8th row 2 more times—80 (88, 98, 106, 114) sts.

Cont in patt until piece measures 12" (30.5 cm) from CO, ending with a WS row.

Shape Armholes

BO 5 (5, 6, 6, 6) sts at beg of next 2 rows—70 (78, 86, 94, 102) sts rem.

NEXT ROW: (RS; dec row) K1, k2tog, work in patt to last 3 sts, ssk, k1—2 sts dec'd.

Rep dec row every RS row 3 (5, 5, 7, 7) more times—62 (66, 74, 78, 86) sts rem.

Work even in patt until armholes measure 7 (7½, 8, 8½, 9)" (18 [19, 20.5, 21.5, 23] cm), ending with a WS row.

Shape Shoulders

BO 1 st at beg of next 2 rows—60 (64, 72, 76, 84) sts rem.

BO 2 sts at beg of next 4 (6, 6, 8, 10) rows—52 (52, 60, 60, 64) sts rem. BO all sts.

Front

With cir needle and MC, CO 80 (88, 98, 106, 114) sts. Do not join.

NEXT ROW: (RS) K23 (27, 32, 36, 40), pm, work 34 sts according to Row 1 of Cable chart, pm, knit to end.

Work 1 WS row in patt.

Shape Pocket Openings

NEXT ROW: (RS; dec row) K1, sssk (see Glossary), work in patt to last 4 sts, k3tog, k1—4 sts dec'd.

Rep dec row every RS row once more—72 (80, 90, 98, 106) sts rem. Work even in patt until piece measures 4½" (11.5 cm) from CO, ending with a WS row.

NEXT ROW: (RS; inc row) K1, M1, work in patt to last st, M1, k1—2 sts inc'd.

Rep inc row every RS row 3 more times and *at the same time,* when piece measures 5" (12.5 cm) from CO, shape waist as for back.

Work as for back until armhole measures 5 (5½, 6, 6½, 7)" (12.5 [14, 15, 16.5, 18] cm), ending with a WS row.

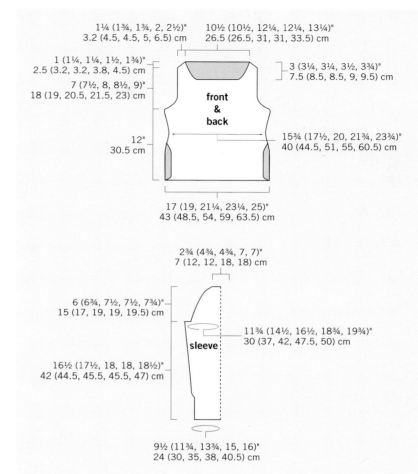

1¼ (1¾, 1¾, 2, 2½)"
3.2 (4.5, 4.5, 5, 6.5) cm

10½ (10½, 12¼, 12¼, 13¼)"
26.5 (26.5, 31, 31, 33.5) cm

1 (1¼, 1¼, 1½, 1¾)"
2.5 (3.2, 3.2, 3.8, 4.5) cm

3 (3¼, 3¼, 3½, 3¾)"
7.5 (8.5, 8.5, 9, 9.5) cm

7 (7½, 8, 8½, 9)"
18 (19, 20.5, 21.5, 23) cm

front & back

12"
30.5 cm

15¾ (17½, 20, 21¾, 23¾)"
40 (44.5, 51, 55, 60.5) cm

17 (19, 21¼, 23¼, 25)"
43 (48.5, 54, 59, 63.5) cm

2¾ (4¾, 4¾, 7, 7)"
7 (12, 12, 18, 18) cm

6 (6¾, 7½, 7½, 7¾)"
15 (17, 19, 19, 19.5) cm

11¾ (14½, 16½, 18¾, 19¾)"
30 (37, 42, 47.5, 50) cm

sleeve

16½ (17½, 18, 18, 18½)"
42 (44.5, 45.5, 45.5, 47) cm

9½ (11¾, 13¾, 15, 16)"
24 (30, 35, 38, 40.5) cm

Shape Neck

NEXT ROW: (RS) K11 (13, 17, 19, 23), attach a new strand of yarn, BO 40 sts, knit to end—11 (13, 17, 19, 23) sts rem each side.

Work each side separately at the same time.

BO 2 (2, 6, 6, 8) sts at each neck edge once—9 (11, 11, 13, 15) sts rem each side.

Dec 1 st at each neck edge every RS row 4 times—5 (7, 7, 9, 11) sts rem each side.

Work in St st until armholes measure 7 (7½, 8, 8½, 9)" (18 [19, 20.5, 21.5, 23] cm), ending with a WS row.

Shape Shoulders

At each armhole edge, BO 1 st once, then BO 2 sts 2 (3, 3, 4, 5) times—no sts rem.

Sleeves

Note: Sleeves are worked in the rnd until beg of cap shaping, then back and forth to end.

With dpn and MC, CO 36 (44, 52, 56, 60) sts. Pm and join for working in the rnd, being careful not to twist sts.

Work in k2, p2 rib for 25 rnds. Change to St st.

NEXT RND: (inc rnd) Knit, inc 4 (6, 6, 8, 8) sts evenly spaced around—40 (50, 58, 64, 68) sts.

Shape Sleeve

NEXT RND: (inc rnd) K1, M1, knit to last st, M1, k1—2 sts inc'd.

Rep inc rnd every 10th rnd 4 (5, 5, 7, 7) more times—50 (62, 70, 80, 84) sts.

Work even until piece measures 16½ (17½, 18, 18, 18½)" (42 [44.5, 45.5, 45.5, 47] cm) from CO.

Shape Cap

Working back and forth in rows, BO 5 sts at beg of next 2 rows—40 (52, 60, 70, 74) sts rem.

NEXT ROW: (RS; dec row) K1, k2tog, knit to last 3 sts, ssk, k1—2 sts dec'd.

Rep dec row every RS row 3 (5, 7, 7, 7) more times, then every 4th row 4 times, then every 6th row 2 times—20 (28, 32, 42, 46) sts rem. Work 1 WS row even.

NEXT ROW: (RS; dec row) K1, k3tog, knit to last 4 sts, sssk (see Glossary), k1—4 sts dec'd.

Rep last dec row every RS row 1 (1, 2, 2, 3) more time(s)—12 (20, 20, 30, 30) sts rem.

BO all sts.

Finishing

Sew in sleeves. With MC threaded on a tapestry needle, sew side seams from top of pocket shaping to underarm. Sew shoulder seams.

Pockets

With dpn, CC, and RS facing, pick up and knit (see Glossary) 32 sts along front edge of pocket opening, pm, pick up and knit 32 sts along back edge of pocket opening—64 sts total. Pm and join for working in the rnd.

Knit 1 rnd.

Purl 1 rnd.

Knit 1 rnd.

NEXT RND: (dec rnd) *K2, ssk, knit to 4 sts before m, k2tog, k2; rep from * once more—4 sts dec'd.

Knit 1 rnd.

Rep dec rnd—56 sts rem.

Work even in St st until piece measures 2" (5 cm) from pick-up rnd, then rep dec rnd—52 sts rem. Work 1 rnd even. Rep dec rnd—48 sts rem.

Work even in St st until piece measures 3½" (9 cm) from pick-up rnd.

Rep dec rnd every other rnd 3 times—36 sts rem.

Knit 2 rnds. BO all sts. With CC threaded on a tapestry needle, sew BO edge of pocket closed.

Lower Ribbing

With cir needle, MC, and RS facing, pick up and knit 148 (164, 184, 200, 216) sts evenly spaced along bottom edge. Pm and join for working in the rnd. Work in k2, p2 rib for 2½" (6.5 cm). BO all sts in rib.

Cowl

With cir needle, MC, RS facing, and beg at center of back neck, pick up and knit 124 (128, 132, 136, 140) sts evenly spaced around neck opening. Pm and join for working in the rnd.

Work in k2, p2 rib for 1½" (3.8 cm).

NEXT RND: (dec rnd) *K2tog, p2; rep from * to end of rnd—93 (96, 99, 102, 105) sts rem.

Work in k1, p2 rib for 3 rnds.

NEXT RND: (inc rnd) *M1, k1, M1, p2; rep from * to end of rnd—155 (160, 165, 170, 175) sts.

Work in k3, p2 rib until piece measures 6" (15 cm) from pick-up rnd. BO all sts in rib.

Weave in loose ends. Block to measurements.

Back

With MC and smallest needles, CO 70 (78, 86, 94, 102) sts.

SET-UP ROW: (RS) K1, *k4, p4; rep from * to last 5 sts, k5.

NEXT ROW: (WS) Work sts as they appear.

Work in patt as established until piece measures 3½" (9 cm) from CO, ending with a WS row.

Change to St st and work even until piece measures 13 (12½, 12, 11½, 11)" (33 [31.5, 30.5, 29, 28] cm) from CO, ending with a WS row.

Shape Armholes

BO 4 (4, 5, 6, 6) sts at beg of next 2 rows—62 (70, 76, 82, 90) sts rem.

BO 2 (3, 4, 4, 5) sts at beg of next 2 rows—58 (64, 68, 74, 80) sts rem.

NEXT ROW: (RS; dec row) K1, ssk, knit to last 3 sts, k2tog, k1—2 sts dec'd.

Rep dec row every RS row 2 more times—52 (58, 62, 68, 74) sts rem.

Work even until armholes measure 7½ (8, 8½, 9, 9½)" (19 [20.5, 21.5, 23, 24] cm), ending with a WS row.

Shape Shoulders

BO 7 (8, 9, 9, 10) sts at beg of next 2 rows—38 (42, 44, 50, 54) sts rem. BO 6 (7, 8, 8, 9) sts at beg of next 2 rows—26 (28, 28, 34, 36) sts rem. BO all sts.

Left Front

With MC and smallest needles, CO 33 (37, 41, 45, 49) sts.

SET-UP ROW: (RS) P5, *k4, p4; rep from * to last 4 (0, 4, 0, 4) sts, k4 (0, 4, 0, 4).

NEXT ROW: (WS) Work sts as they appear.

Work in patt as established for 3½" (9 cm), ending with a WS row.

Change to St st and work even until piece measures 13 (12½, 12, 11½, 11)" (33 [31.5, 30.5, 29, 28] cm) from CO, ending with a WS row.

Shape Armhole

BO 4 (4, 5, 6, 6) sts at beg of next row—29 (33, 36, 39, 43) sts rem. Work 1 WS row even. BO 2 (3, 4, 4, 5) sts at beg of next row—27 (30, 32, 35, 38) sts rem. Work 1 WS row even.

NEXT ROW: (RS; dec row) K1, ssk, knit to end—1 st dec'd.

Rep dec row every RS row 2 more times—24 (27, 29, 32, 35) sts rem. Work even until armhole measures 6½ (7, 7½, 8, 8½)" (16.5 [18, 19, 20.5, 21.5] cm), ending with a RS row.

Shape Neck

BO 9 (10, 10, 12, 13) sts at beg of next row—15 (17, 19, 20, 22) sts rem. Work 1 RS row even. BO 2 (2, 2, 3, 3) sts at beg of next row—13 (15, 17, 17, 19) sts rem. Work 2 rows even.

Shape Shoulder

BO 7 (8, 9, 9, 10) sts at beg of next RS row—6 (7, 8, 8, 9) sts rem. Work 1 WS row even. BO all sts.

Right Front

With MC and smallest needles, CO 33 (37, 41, 45, 49) sts.

SET-UP ROW: (RS) K4 (0, 4, 0, 4), *p4, k4; rep from * to last 5 sts, p5.

NEXT ROW: (WS) Work sts as they appear.

Work in patt as established for 3½" (9 cm), ending with a WS row.

Change to St st and work even until piece measures 13 (12½, 12, 11½, 11)" (33 [31.5, 30.5, 29, 28] cm) from CO, ending with a RS row.

Shape Armhole

BO 4 (4, 5, 6, 6) sts at beg of next row—29 (33, 36, 39, 43) sts rem. Work 1 RS row even. BO 2

(3, 4, 4, 5) sts at beg of next row—27 (30, 32, 35, 38) sts rem.

NEXT ROW: (RS; dec row) Knit to last 3 sts, k2tog, k1—1 st dec'd.

Rep dec row every RS row 2 more times—24 (27, 29, 32, 35) sts rem. Work even until armhole measures 6½ (7, 7½, 8, 8½)" (16.5 [18, 19, 20.5, 21.5] cm), ending with a WS row.

Shape Neck

BO 9 (10, 10, 12, 13) sts at beg of next row—15 (17, 19, 20, 22) sts rem. Work 1 WS row even. BO 2 (2, 2, 3, 3) sts at beg of next row—13 (15, 17, 17, 19) sts rem. Work 2 rows even.

Shape Shoulder

BO 7 (8, 9, 9, 10) sts at beg of next WS row—6 (7, 8, 8, 9) sts rem. Work 1 RS row even. BO all sts.

Sleeves

With MC and smallest needles, CO 34 (38, 38, 42, 42) sts.

SET-UP ROW: (RS) K1, *k4, p4; rep from * to last 1 (5, 5, 1, 1) st(s), p1 (0, 0, 1, 1), k0 (5, 5, 0, 0).

NEXT ROW: (WS) Work sts as they appear.

Work even in patt as established until piece measures 2½" (6.5 cm) from CO, ending with a WS row.

Shape Sleeve

Change to St st.

NEXT ROW: (RS) K1, M1 (see Glossary), knit to last 2 sts, M1, k2—2 sts inc'd.

Rep inc row every 6th row 0 (0, 4, 4, 12) more times, then every 8th row 6 (6, 8, 8, 2) times, then every 10th row 4 (4, 0, 0, 0) times—56 (60, 64, 68, 72) sts.

Work even in St st until piece measures 18" (45.5 cm) from CO, ending with a WS row.

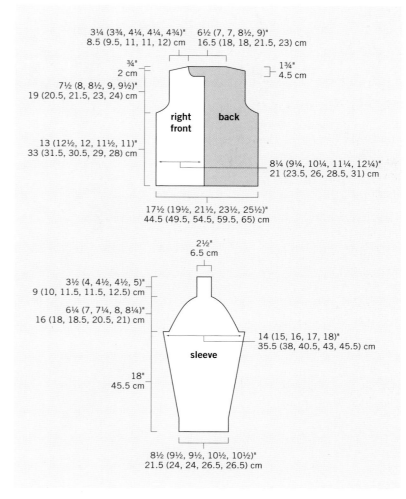

3¼ (3¾, 4¼, 4¼, 4¾)"
8.5 (9.5, 11, 11, 12) cm

6½ (7, 7, 8½, 9)"
16.5 (18, 18, 21.5, 23) cm

¾"
2 cm

1¾"
4.5 cm

7½ (8, 8½, 9, 9½)"
19 (20.5, 21.5, 23, 24) cm

right
front   back

13 (12½, 12, 11½, 11)"
33 (31.5, 30.5, 29, 28) cm

8¼ (9¼, 10¼, 11¼, 12¼)"
21 (23.5, 26, 28.5, 31) cm

17½ (19½, 21½, 23½, 25½)"
44.5 (49.5, 54.5, 59.5, 65) cm

2½"
6.5 cm

3½ (4, 4½, 4½, 5)"
9 (10, 11.5, 11.5, 12.5) cm

6¼ (7, 7¼, 8, 8¼)"
16 (18, 18.5, 20.5, 21) cm

14 (15, 16, 17, 18)"
35.5 (38, 40.5, 43, 45.5) cm

sleeve

18"
45.5 cm

8½ (9½, 9½, 10½, 10½)"
21.5 (24, 24, 26.5, 26.5) cm

Shape Cap

BO 4 (4, 5, 6, 6) sts at beg of next 2 rows—48 (52, 54, 56, 60) sts rem. BO 2 (3, 4, 4, 5) sts at beg of next 2 rows—44 (46, 46, 48, 50) sts rem.

NEXT ROW: (RS; dec row) K1, ssk, knit to last 3 sts, k2tog, k1—2 sts dec'd.

Rep dec row every RS row 1 more time, then every 4th row 3 (4, 5, 6, 6) times, then every RS row 4 (4, 3, 3, 4) times—26 sts rem. Work 1 WS row even. BO 2 sts at beg of next 8 rows—10 sts rem.

Saddle Shoulder

Work even for 3½ (4, 4½, 4½, 5)" (9 [10, 11.5, 11.5, 12.5] cm), ending with a WS row. BO all sts.

Front Panel

With MC and middle-size needles, CO 22 sts. Knit 3 rows. Change to largest needles. Work Fair Isle chart. Knit 1 RS row. Change to middle-size needles. Knit 3 rows. BO all sts.

Right Panel Edge Trim

With RS facing, MC, and middle-size needles, pick up and knit (see Glossary) 46 sts along right edge of panel.

Knit 1 WS row.

NEXT ROW: (RS; beg buttonhole row) K4, BO 2 sts, *k10, BO 2 sts; rep from * 2 more times, k4.

NEXT ROW: (WS; end buttonhole row) *Knit to BO sts, using the backward-loop method (see Glossary), CO 2 sts; rep from * 3 more times, knit to end of row.

Knit 2 rows. BO all sts.

Left Panel Edge Trim

Work as for right panel edge trim, picking up sts along left edge of panel.

Finishing

Block pieces to measurements.

With yarn threaded on a tapestry needle, sew front and back shoulders to sides of saddle at top of sleeves. Sew in sleeves. Sew side and sleeve seams.

Collar

With smallest needles, MC, and RS facing, pick up and knit 16 (17, 17, 20, 21) sts along right front neck, 10 sts along saddle shoulder, 26 (28, 28, 34, 36) sts along back neck, 10 sts along saddle

fair isle

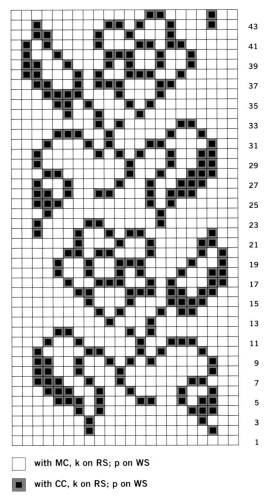

☐ with MC, k on RS; p on WS

■ with CC, k on RS; p on WS

shoulder, and 16 (17, 17, 20, 21) sts along left front neck—78 (82, 82, 94, 98) sts total.

NEXT ROW: (WS) P1 (3, 3, 1, 3), *k4, p4; rep from * to last 5 (7, 7, 5, 7) sts, k4, p1 (3, 3, 1, 3).

NEXT ROW: (RS) Work sts as they appear.

Work in patt as established until piece measures 1" (2.5 cm) from pick-up row, ending with a WS row.

NEXT ROW: (RS; dec row) K1 (3, 3, 1, 3), *p1, p2tog, p1, k4; rep from * to last 5 (7, 7, 5, 7) sts, p1, p2tog, p1, k1 (3, 3, 1, 3)—68 (72, 72, 82, 86) sts rem.

NEXT ROW: (WS) Work sts as they appear.

Work even in rib patt until piece measures 2¼" (5.5 cm) from pick-up row, ending with a WS row. BO all sts in patt.

Front Bands

With MC, smallest needles, and RS facing, pick up and knit 87 sts along left front edge.

ROW 1: (WS) Purl.

ROW 2: *K1, sl 1 pwise with yarn in back (wyb); rep from * to last st, k1.

Rep Rows 1 and 2 two more times. With WS facing, BO all sts kwise.

Rep for right front edge.

Attach Snaps

With RS of left front band facing, sew bottom of one snap ¼" (6 mm) below top of band. Sew bottom of another snap 1" (2.5 cm) above bottom edge. Sew rem snap bottoms evenly spaced between top and bottom snaps. On WS of right front band, sew snap tops opposite snap bottoms.

Attach Buttons

Center front panel 2½" (6.5 cm) below pick-up row for collar. Mark button placement on left and right fronts to correspond with buttonholes. Sew on buttons.

Weave in loose ends.

providence
HOODIE

DESIGNER
Melissa LaBarre

The braided cable that forms the bottom edge of this classic hooded cardigan is repeated on the hood, and an allover moss-stitch pattern adds rich texture as well as warmth. Whether the front is buttoned against a wind or the hood is thrown back, this is a sweater for all seasons.

finished size

30½ (35, 38½, 43, 46½, 51)" (77.5 [89, 98, 109, 118, 129.5] cm) bust circumference, buttoned; sweater shown measures 35" (89 cm).

YARN

Worsted (Medium #4).

shown here: Vermont Organic Fiber Company O-Wool Classic (100% merino; 198 yd [181 m]/100 g): #7100 oatmeal, 6 (7, 8, 9, 9, 10) skeins.

NEEDLES

U.S. size 8 (5 mm): 40" (100 cm) circular (cir) and set of 4 or 5 double-pointed (dpn). Adjust needle size if necessary to obtain the correct gauge.

NOTIONS

Markers (m); stitch holders or waste yarn; cable needle (cn); six 1" (2.5 cm) buttons; tapestry needle.

GAUGE

18 sts and 28 rows = 4" (10 cm) in moss st.

NEXT ROW: (RS; inc row) *Work in patt to 2 sts before m, M1R (see Glossary), k2, sl m, k2, M1L (see Glossary); rep from * once more, work in patt to end—4 sts inc'd.

Rep inc row every 6th row 4 more times, working new sts into moss st—135 (153, 171, 189, 207, 225) sts.

Work even in patt until piece measures 15½" (39.5 cm) from bottom of cable panel, ending with a RS row.

NEXT ROW: (WS) *Work in patt to 4 (4, 4, 4, 6, 8) sts before m, BO 4 (4, 4, 4, 6, 8) sts, remove m, BO 4 (4, 4, 4, 6, 8) sts; rep from * once more, work in patt to end—119 (137, 155, 173, 183, 193) sts rem; 29 (33, 38, 42, 45, 47) sts for each front, 61 (71, 79, 89, 93, 99) sts for back.

Join Sleeves and Body

NEXT ROW: (RS) Work in patt to 2 sts before BO sts, work 2 sts in St st, pm, work 2 sleeve sts in St st, work in moss st to last 2 sts of sleeve, work 2 sleeve sts in St st, pm, work 2 back sts in St st, work in moss st to 2 sts before BO sts, work 2 sts in St st, pm, work 2 sleeve sts in St st, work in moss st to last 2 sts of sleeve, work 2 sleeve sts in St st, pm, work 2 front sts in St st, work in patt to end—199 (225, 251, 273, 279, 285) sts.

Work 1 row in patt as established.

Shape Raglan

ROW 1: (RS; dec row) *Work in patt to 3 sts before m, k2tog, k1, sl m, k1, ssk; rep from * 3 more times, work in patt to end—8 sts dec'd.

ROW 2: Work even, keeping 2 sts each side of each m in St st.

Rep last 2 rows 10 (12, 14, 16, 16, 15) more times—111 (121, 131, 137, 143, 157) sts rem; 18 (20, 23, 25, 28, 31) sts for each front, 39 (45, 49, 55, 59, 67) sts for back, and 18 (18, 18, 16, 14, 14) sts for each sleeve.

Shape Neck and Raglan

Note: Raglan decs cont on RS rows at the same time as neck shaping.

NEXT ROW: (RS; dec row) K2, ssk, *work in patt to 3 sts before m, k2tog, k1, sl m, k1, ssk; rep from * 3 more times, work in patt to last 4 sts, k2tog, k2—10 sts dec'd.

Rep dec row every RS row 4 more times—61 (71, 81, 87, 93, 107) sts rem; 8 (10, 13, 15, 18, 21) sts for each front, 29 (35, 39, 45, 49, 57) sts for back, and 8 (8, 8, 6, 4, 4) sts for each sleeve.

Change to St st. Work 3 rows even, ending with a WS row and removing raglan markers.

Hood

NEXT ROW: (RS) K3, pm, k17 (27, 37, 35, 32, 25), [k1f&b] 21 (11, 1, 0, 0, 0) times, [k2tog] 0 (0, 0, 5, 11, 25) times, knit to last 3 sts, pm, k3—82 sts.

Purl 1 WS row.

NEXT ROW: (RS) K3, work Row 1 of cable patt to last 3 sts, k3.

Work in patt as established, working first and last 3 sts in St st and sts between m in cable patt, until cable section measures 12" (30.5 cm) or desired length, ending with a WS row.

NEXT ROW: (RS; dec row) K39, k2tog, ssk, knit to end—80 sts rem.

NEXT ROW: (WS) P3, k2, purl to 2 sts before m, k2, p3.

NEXT ROW: (RS; dec row) K38, k2tog, ssk, knit to end—78 sts rem.

Sl 39 sts to right needle. With RS tog, 1 dpn, and using the three-needle method (see Glossary), BO all sts.

Finishing

Sew underarm seams.

Front Band

With cir needle and RS facing, beg at right front lower edge, pick up and knit 102 (105, 108, 112, 112, 109) sts to beg of neck shaping, 13 sts to beg of hood, 57 sts to center hood seam, 57 sts from center hood seam to end of hood, 13 sts to end of neck shaping, and 102 (105, 108, 112, 112, 109) sts to left front lower edge—344 (350, 356, 364, 364, 358) sts total. Work in moss st for 5 rows.

NEXT ROW: (RS; buttonhole row) Work 4 sts in patt, k2tog, yo, *work 16 sts in patt, k2tog, yo; rep from * 4 more times, work in moss st to end of row.

Work 4 rows in moss st. With WS facing, BO all sts kwise. Weave in loose ends. Block to measurements.

Sew buttons to left front band opposite buttonholes.

along
THE COAST

The lovely and diverse coastlines of New England are one of the biggest draws for visitors—and one of the favorite features of those who live there. Sandy and rocky beaches, boardwalks lined with boats, and trails through wildlife preserves provide wonderful water views. A stroll along the water can be lovely, serene, and calm, as long as you are dressed for the weather. The garments in this section are meant for those last fall walks by the ocean before the weather turns too cold or even an outing at the first light of morning before the sun warms the air. Close-fitting wool vests, a versatile scarf, and a sweater with a lace yoke will keep the coastal winds at bay while you take in the view.

salem
HOODED JACKET

DESIGNER
Melissa LaBarre

The built-in pockets and cozy hood of this simple round-yoked cardigan give a little extra warmth. Two rows of eyelets around the yoke provide a channel for ribbon or an I-cord to be threaded through and tied at each end. The hidden snaps at the neck allow the jacket to hang open in an A shape.

finished size
34½ (37½, 41, 44½, 48)" (87.5 [95, 104, 113, 122] cm) bust circumference with jacket closed; jacket shown measures 34½" (87.5 cm).

YARN
Worsted (Medium #4).

shown here: Manos del Uruguay Wool Clásica (100% wool; 138 yd [126 m]/100 g): #64 pewter, 7 (8, 9, 10, 10) skeins.

NEEDLES
U.S. size 10 (6 mm): 32" (80 cm) and 16" (40 cm) circular (cir) and set of 4 or 5 double-pointed (dpn). Adjust needle size if necessary to obtain the correct gauge.

NOTIONS
3 markers (m); 1 removable marker; stitch holders or waste yarn; 2 sew-on snaps; matching sewing thread and needle; tapestry needle; 2¼ yd [2 m] of ⅝" (1.5 cm) ribbon.

GAUGE
14 sts and 24 rows = 4" (10 cm) in St st.

Neck and Hood

NEXT ROW: (RS) BO 14 sts, remove m, work 14 sts in box st, pm, work in St st to last 28 sts and *at the same time* dec 3 (3, 3, 3, 4) sts in St st section, pm, work in box st to end—77 (89, 99, 111, 121) sts rem.

NEXT ROW: (WS) BO 14 sts, remove m, work in patt to end—63 (75, 85, 97, 107) sts rem.

Pm in center st of hood.

Cont in patt, working St st for hood and keeping first and last 14 sts in box st, until hood measures 10" (25.5 cm), ending with a WS row.

NEXT ROW: (RS; dec row) Work to 2 sts before marked center st, k2tog, k1 (center st), ssk, work in patt to end—2 sts dec'd.

Rep dec row every 4th row once more, then every RS row once—57 (69, 79, 91, 101) sts rem.

Work even in patt until hood measures 12" (30.5 cm) or desired length. Sl 29 (34, 39, 45, 50) sts to 1 dpn and fold hood so needles are parallel with RS tog. With WS facing, use the three-needle method (see Glossary) to BO all sts, working 2 sts tog at end of one needle.

Finishing

Pockets

Pocket lining
With RS facing, pick up and knit 1 st in each CO pocket st—20 sts total. Work in St st until lining measures 3½" (9 cm), ending with a WS row. BO all sts.

Pocket flap
Place 20 held pocket sts onto needle. With RS facing, attach yarn and work in box st for 10 rows. BO all sts. Use running st (see Glossary) to sew down sides of pocket flap, lining, and bottom of pocket. Rep for second pocket.

Beg at left front edge, fold ribbon in half and thread one half through upper row of eyelets and other half through lower row. Tie ends of ribbon in

a bow on right front (with sweater on the recipient, to keep from tightening the yoke).

Place held underarm sts onto 2 dpn. With RS tog, use the three-needle method to BO underarm sts.

Weave in loose ends. With sewing needle and thread, sew bottom halves of snaps to top corners of left front box st panel, then sew top halves to underside of right front box st panel.

Block to measurements.

derry
RAGLAN and COWL

DESIGNER
Cecily Glowik MacDonald

For the ultimate in transitional-weather knitting, this raglan pullover
has an optional knitted cowl that keeps a chill off your neck when the
temperatures drop. In warmer weather, the simple neckline and lace
panels on the sleeves allow in a little fresh air. The tweedy texture
and lace panels make it especially fun to knit.

finished size

34 (38, 42, 46, 49, 53, 56)" (86.5 [96.5, 106.5, 117, 124.5, 134.5, 142] cm)
bust circumference; sweater shown measures 38" (96.5 cm). *Cowl:* 25½" (65 cm)
circumference and 7" (18 cm) tall.

YARN

Worsted (Medium #4).

shown here: Karabella Soft Tweed
(100% wool; 108 yd [99 m]/50 g):
#1310 light blue, 7 (8, 9, 10, 10,
11, 12) balls for sweater, 2 balls for
cowl.

NEEDLES

U.S. size 7 (4.5 mm): 16" (40 cm)
and 29" (73.5 cm) circular (cir) and
set of 4 or 5 double-pointed (dpn).
Adjust needle size if necessary to
obtain the correct gauge.

NOTIONS

Markers (m; 1 color for beg of rnd, 3
of one color for raglan shaping, 4 of
another color for lace panels); stitch
holders or waste yarn; tapestry needle.

GAUGE

16 sts and 25 rows = 4" (10 cm) in
St st.

Sweater

Yoke

With shorter cir needle, CO 30 sts, place marker (pm) for raglan, CO 11 sts, pm for raglan, CO 30 sts, pm for raglan, CO 11 sts—82 sts total. Pm and join for working in the rnd, being careful not to twist sts.

NEXT RND: (inc rnd) *K1, LLI (see Glossary), work in St st to 2 sts before raglan m, RLI (see Glossary), k1, sl m, k1, LLI, k1, pm for beg of lace panel, work 7 sts according to Lace Panel chart, pm for end of lace panel, RLI, k1, sl m; rep from * once more—90 sts. *Note:* Sts between lace panel markers will be worked in lace patt to cuff; other sts are worked in St st.

Work 1 rnd even in patt.

even rows— no increa

NEXT RND: (inc rnd) *K1, LLI, work in patt to 2 sts before raglan m, RLI, k1, sl m; rep from * to end—8 sts inc'd.

Rep inc rnd every other rnd 6 (12, 17, 21, 23, 25, 27) more times, then every 4th rnd 9 (7, 4, 2, 0, 0, 0) times—218 (250, 266, 282, 282, 298, 314) sts. Work 1 rnd even.

Raglan - K & 1 stitch B4 M, yo K1, SM, K1, yo, K & ...

Schematic measurements

20½"
52 cm

1¼"
3.2 cm

12¼ (14¼, 15¼, 16¼, 16¼, 17¼, 18¼)"
31 (36, 38.5, 41.5, 41.5, 44, 46.5) cm

8¼ (9, 9, 9¾, 10, 11¼, 12¼)"
21 (23, 23, 25, 25.5, 28.5, 31) cm

pullover

7¾ (8¾, 9¾, 10¾, 9¾, 10¾, 11¾)"
19.5 (22, 25, 27.5, 25, 27.5, 30) cm

19"
48.5 cm

12½ (12, 11½, 11, 10½, 10, 9½)"
31.5 (30.5, 29, 28, 26.5, 25.5, 24) cm

30 (34, 38, 42, 45, 49, 52)"
76 (86.5, 96.5, 106.5, 114.5, 124.5, 132) cm

34 (38, 42, 46, 49, 53, 56)"
86.5 (96.5, 106.5, 117, 124.5, 134.5, 142) cm

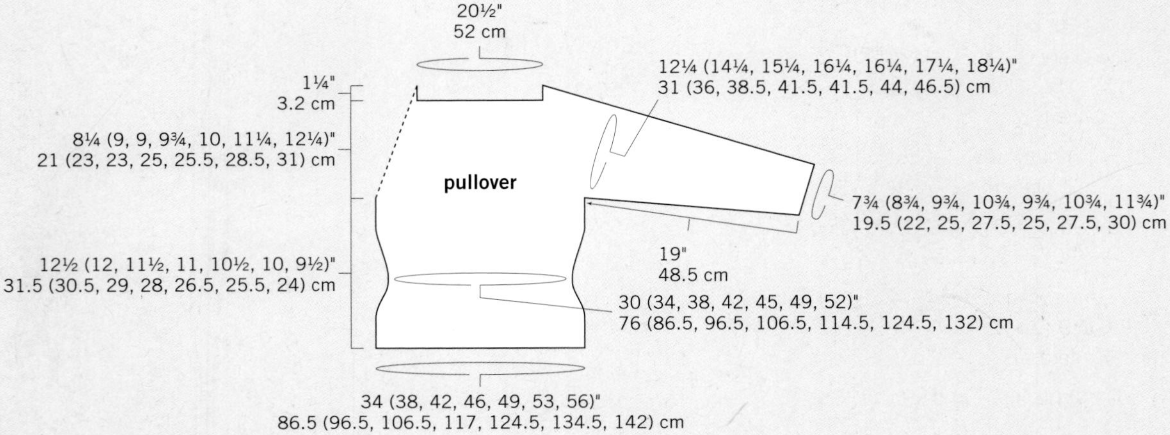

Sizes 42 (46, 49, 53, 56)"
(106.5 [117, 124.5, 134.5, 142] cm) only
Work raglan shaping on front and back only as foll:

NEXT RND: (body inc rnd) *K1, LLI, work to 2 sts before next raglan m, RLI, k1, sl m, work in patt to next raglan m, sl m; rep from * once more—4 sts inc'd.

Rep body inc rnd every other rnd 1 (3, 6, 8, 9) more time(s)—274 (298, 310, 334, 354) sts.

All sizes
Change to longer cir needle when there are too many sts to work comfortably on shorter needle.

Divide for Body and Sleeves

Work 64 (72, 80, 88, 94, 102, 108) sts for back, removing m as you come to them, place 45 (53, 57, 61, 61, 65, 69) sts on holder for right sleeve, CO 2 sts, pm for side, CO 2 sts, work 64 (72, 80, 88, 94, 102, 108) sts for front, place 45 (53, 57, 61, 61, 65, 69) sts on holder for left sleeve, CO 2 sts, pm for beg of rnd, CO 2 sts, join for working in the rnd—136 (152, 168, 184, 196, 212, 224) body sts. Work even until piece measures 2½ (2, 1, 1½, 1, ½, ½)" (6.5 [5, 2.5, 3.8, 2.5, 1.3, 1.3] cm) from underarm.

Shape Waist

NEXT RND: (dec rnd) *K2tog, work to 2 sts before m, ssk, sl m; rep from * once more—4 sts dec'd.

Rep dec rnd every 6th rnd 0 (0, 0, 0, 3, 3, 3) more times, then every 8th rnd 3 (3, 3, 3, 0, 0, 0) times—120 (136, 152, 168, 180, 196, 208) sts rem. Work 3 rnds even.

NEXT RND: (inc rnd) *LLI, work to 1 st before m, RLI, sl m; rep from * once more—4 sts inc'd.

Rep inc rnd every 6th rnd 3 more times—136 (152, 168, 184, 196, 212, 224) sts.

Work even until piece measures 11½ (11, 10½, 10, 9½, 9, 8½)" (29 [28, 26.5, 25.5, 24, 23, 21.5] cm) from underarm.

Work even in k2, p2 rib for 1" (2.5 cm). BO all sts in patt.

lace panel

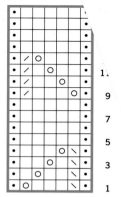

knit

· purl

o yo

∕ k2tog

∖ ssk

☐ pattern repeat

Sleeves
Place 45 (53, 57, 61, 61, 65, 69) sleeve...
CO 2 sts, pm for b...
Attach yarn for working in the rnd...
dpn. Work 4 rnds...
2 sts, join to establish...
65, 69, 73) sts...
Lace Panel as established...
NEXT RND: (dec r...
m, ssk—2 st...
Rep dec...
mo...

sts onto
_g of rnd, CO
—49 (57, 61, 65,
even in St st with
ed.

d) K2tog, work to 2 sts before
dec'd.

rnd every 12th rnd 8 (0, 0, 0, 0, 0, 0)
times, every 10th rnd 0 (8, 8, 8, 5, 5, 5)
times, every 8th rnd 0 (2, 2, 2, 2, 2, 2) times,
then every 6th rnd 0 (0, 0, 0, 5, 5, 5) times—31
(35, 39, 43, 39, 43, 47) sts rem.

Work even in patt until piece measures 18" (45.5
cm) from underarm.

Rib

NEXT RND: Remove m's for Lace Panel as you
come to them. K1, *k2, p2; rep from * to last 2
sts, p2. Work even in rib as established for 1" (2.5
cm). BO all sts in patt.

Finishing

Block piece to measurements. Sew underarm
seams.

With shorter cir needle, pick up and knit (see Glossary) 82 sts evenly spaced around neck. With RS
facing, BO all sts. Weave in loose ends.

Cowl

With shorter cir needle, CO 102 sts. Pm and join
for working in the rnd, being careful not to twist
sts.

NEXT RND: (set-up rnd) *K10, work 7 sts according to Lace Panel chart; rep from * to end.

Work even in patt as established until piece measures 7" (18 cm) from CO, ending with Row 4 or
12 of patt. BO all sts in patt.

Weave in loose ends.

old port
PULLOVER

DESIGNER
Kristen TenDyke

Kristen TenDyke's pullover proves that a sweater can be cozy but still feminine. The cables emphasize the figure-flattering silhouette, including the elegant waist shaping. The lace pattern keeps the sweater from being too bulky. The sweater is worked with no seams, so it's ready to wear when you've finished knitting.

finished size

28¼ (33, 37¾, 42½, 47¼, 52)" (72 [84, 96, 108, 120, 132] cm) bust circumference; sweater shown measures 33" (84 cm).

YARN

Worsted (Medium #4).

shown here: Classic Elite Princess (40% merino, 28% viscose, 15% nylon, 10% cashmere, 7% angora; 150 yd [137 m]/50 g): #3405 vintage rose, 7 (7, 8, 10, 11, 12) balls.

NEEDLES

U.S. sizes 6 and 7 (4 and 4.5 mm): one 24 (24, 24, 36, 36, 36)" (60 [60, 60, 90, 90, 90] cm) circular (cir) and set of 4 or 5 double-pointed (dpn). Adjust needle size if necessary to obtain the correct gauge.

NOTIONS

Cable needle (cn); markers (m; 1 of one color for beg of rnd, 1 of another color for side of body, and 4 of a third color for waist and sleeve shaping); stitch holders or waste yarn; tapestry needle.

GAUGE

22 sts and 28 rnds = 4" (10 cm) in Cable Rib patt on larger needle.

NOTE

A cable runs up the inside of each sleeve; stitches are increased on each side of this cable.

Body

With smaller cir needle, CO 144 (168, 192, 216, 240, 264) sts. Place marker (pm) and join for working in the rnd, being careful not to twist sts.

RNDS 1 AND 2: *K2, p1; rep from * to end.

RND 3: (inc rnd) *K2, p1, k2, M1P (see Glossary), p1, [k2, p1] 2 times; rep from * to end—156 (182, 208, 234, 260, 286) sts.

Change to larger cir needle and work Cable Rib chart until piece measures 3 (3, 3½, 3½, 4, 4)" (7.5 [7.5, 9, 9, 10, 10] cm) from CO.

NEXT RND: Work 29 (29, 42, 42, 55, 55) sts in patt, pm, work 32 sts in patt, pm, work 17 (30, 30, 43, 43, 56) sts in patt, pm for side; rep from * once more.

Shape Waist

NEXT RND: (dec rnd) *Work to 3 sts before m, ssk or ssp keeping in patt, p1, sl m, work to next m, sl m, p1, k2tog or p2tog keeping in patt, work to next m, sl m; rep from * once more—4 sts dec'd.

Rep dec rnd every 6th rnd once more, then every 8th rnd 2 times—140 (166, 192, 218, 244, 270) sts rem.

Work 9 rnds even.

NEXT RND: (dec rnd) *Work to 3 sts before m, sl 1 kwise with yarn in front (wyf), p2tog, psso, sl m, work to next m, sl m, sl 1 kwise wyf, p2tog, psso, work to next m, sl m; rep from * once more—132 (158, 184, 210, 236, 262) sts rem.

Work even in patt until piece measures 10 (10½, 11, 11, 11½, 11¾)" (25.5 [26.5, 28, 28, 29, 30] cm) from CO.

NEXT RND: (inc rnd) *Work to 1 st before m, M1P, k1, M1P, sl m, work to next m, sl m, M1P,

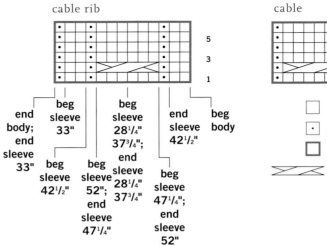

cable rib

cable

□ knit

· purl

□ pattern repeat

⬚ sl 3 sts onto cn, hold in back, k3, k3 from cn

k1, M1P, work to next m, sl m; rep from * once more—140 (166, 192, 218, 244, 270) sts.

Work 7 rnds even.

NEXT RND: (inc rnd) *Work to 1 st before m, LLI (see Glossary), p1, sl m, work to next m, sl m, p1, RLI (see Glossary), work to next m, sl m; rep from * once more—4 sts inc'd.

Rep inc rnd every 6th rnd 3 more times, working new sts into Cable Rib patt—156 (182, 208, 234, 260, 286) sts.

Remove waist markers, keeping beg of rnd and side markers in place. Work even in patt until piece measures about 14¼ (14¾, 15¼, 15½, 16, 16½)" (36 [37.5, 38.5, 39.5, 40.5, 42] cm) from CO, ending with Row 5 (2, 5, 2, 5, 2) of Cable Rib chart, and ending last rnd 0 (2, 0, 2, 0, 2) sts before end of rnd.

Sizes 28¼ (37¾, 47¼)" (72 [96, 120] cm) only

NEXT RND: Working Row 6 of Cable Rib chart, remove m for beg of rnd, work 6 sts in patt, replace m for beg of rnd, work to side m, remove side m, work 6 sts in patt, replace side m, work to last 2 (4, 4) sts of rnd; end here, leaving rem 2 (4, 4) sts unworked—markers are now in center of cables.

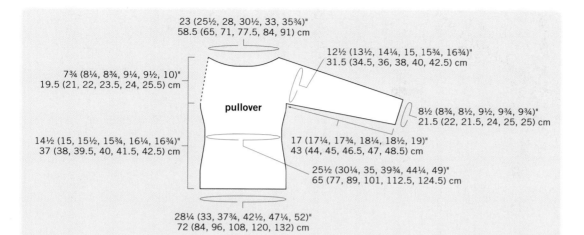

23 (25½, 28, 30½, 33, 35¾)"
58.5 (65, 71, 77.5, 84, 91) cm

12½ (13½, 14¼, 15, 15¾, 16¾)"
31.5 (34.5, 36, 38, 40, 42.5) cm

7¾ (8¼, 8¾, 9¼, 9½, 10)"
19.5 (21, 22, 23.5, 24, 25.5) cm

pullover

8½ (8¾, 8½, 9½, 9¾, 9¾)"
21.5 (22, 21.5, 24, 25, 25) cm

14½ (15, 15½, 15¾, 16¼, 16¾)"
37 (38, 39.5, 40, 41.5, 42.5) cm

17 (17¼, 17¾, 18¼, 18½, 19)"
43 (44, 45, 46.5, 47, 48.5) cm

25½ (30¼, 35, 39¾, 44¼, 49)"
65 (77, 89, 101, 112.5, 124.5) cm

28¼ (33, 37¾, 42½, 47¼, 52)"
72 (84, 96, 108, 120, 132) cm

Sizes 33 (42½, 52)"
(84 [108, 132] cm) only

NEXT RND: (dec rnd) Working Row 3 of Cable Rib chart, ssk, sl m for beg of rnd, work to 2 sts before side m, ssk, sl m, work to 3 sts before end of rnd; end here, leaving rem 3 sts unworked—180 (232, 284) sts rem.

All sizes
Break yarn. Leave sts on needle; set aside.

Sleeves

With smaller dpn, CO 42 (42, 42, 48, 48, 48) sts. Pm and join for working in the rnd, being careful not to twist sts.

RNDS 1 AND 2: *P1, k2; rep from * to end.

Sizes 28¼ (37¾)" (72 [96] cm) only

NEXT RND: (inc rnd) P1, k2, M1, p1, k2, p1, M1, k2, [p1, k2] 3 times, M1, *[p1, k2] 4 times, M1; rep from * once more—47 sts.

Size 33" (84 cm) only

NEXT RND: (inc rnd) P1, k2, M1, p1, k2, p1, M1P, k2, p1, k2, M1, *[p1, k2] 4 times, M1; rep from * once more, [p1, k2] 2 times, M1P—48 sts.

Size 42½" (108 cm) only

NEXT RND: (inc rnd) P1, k2, M1, *[p1, k2] 4 times, M1; rep from * 2 more times, [p1, k2] 3 times—52 sts.

Size 47¼" (120 cm) only

NEXT RND: (inc rnd) P1, k2, M1, [p1, k2] 2 times, *M1, [p1, k2] 4 times; rep from * 2 more times, M1, p1, k2—53 sts.

Size 52" (132 cm) only

NEXT RND: (inc rnd) P1, k2, M1, p1, k2, p1, M1P, k2, [p1, k2] 2 times, M1, *[p1, k2] 4 times, M1; rep from * once more, [p1, k2] 3 times, M1P—54 sts.

All sizes

Change to larger dpn. Work 8 sts according to Cable chart, pm of a different color, beg and ending as indicated for your size, work according to Cable Rib chart to end of rnd. *Note:* If 6 sts are not available for a cable, work sts in St st instead.

Work even until piece measures 3" (7.5 cm) from CO.

Shape Sleeve

NEXT RND: (inc rnd) Work 8 sts in patt, sl m, M1 or M1P keeping in Cable Rib patt, work in patt to end, M1 or M1P keeping in Cable Rib patt, sl m—2 sts inc'd.

Rep inc rnd every 12th rnd 2 (0, 0, 0, 0, 0) more times, every 10th rnd 2 (3, 1, 2, 1, 0) time(s), every 8th rnd 6 (6, 2, 3, 3, 3) times, every 6th rnd 0 (3, 12, 9, 12, 9) times, then every 4th rnd 0 (0, 0, 0, 0, 6) times—69 (74, 79, 82, 87, 92) sts.

Work even in patt until piece measures about 17 (17¼, 17¾, 18¼, 18½, 19)" (43 [44, 45, 46.5, 47, 48.5] cm) from CO, ending with Row 6 (3, 6, 3, 6, 3) of Cable Rib chart. Work 2 (1, 0, 1, 0, 1) sts of next rnd. Break yarn, leaving an 18" (45.5 cm) tail. Place sts on holder.

Yoke

Place next 4 (6, 8, 6, 8, 6) body sts onto holder for underarm, removing m for beg of rnd, join yarn, work in patt to 2 (3, 4, 3, 4, 3) sts before side m, place next 4 (6, 8, 6, 8, 6) sts onto holder for underarm, removing side m, place first 4 (6, 8, 6, 8, 6) sleeve sts onto holder for underarm, pm for raglan, work in patt to end of sleeve, pm for raglan, work in patt to end of body, place first 4 (6, 8, 6, 8, 6) sleeve sts onto holder for underarm, pm for raglan, work in patt to end of sleeve, pm for beg of rnd—278 (304, 334, 372, 402, 444) sts; 74 (84, 96, 110, 122, 136) sts for each of front and back, 65 (68, 71, 76, 79, 86) sts each sleeve.

Shape Yoke

NEXT RND: (dec rnd) *Ssk, work to 2 sts before m, k2tog, sl m; rep from * 3 more times—8 sts dec'd.

Rep dec rnd every rnd 4 (2, 2, 3, 4, 2) more times, then every other rnd 0 (0, 0, 1, 2, 7) time(s)—238 (280, 310, 332, 346, 364) sts rem; 64 (78, 90, 100, 108, 116) sts for each of back and front; 55 (62, 65, 66, 65, 66) sts each sleeve.

Sizes 28¼ (33)" (72 [84] cm) only

Work 1 (0) rnd even.

NEXT RND: (dec rnd) *Work to m, ssk, work to 2 sts before m, k2tog, sl m; rep from * once more—4 sleeve sts dec'd.

yoke

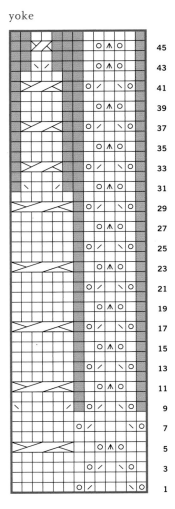
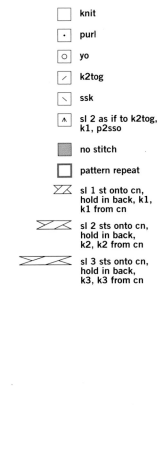

Rep dec rnd every rnd 0 (2) more times, then every other rnd 0 (2) times—234 (260) sts rem; 64 (78) sts each back and front; 53 (52) sts each sleeve.

*Sizes 37¾ (42½, 47¼)"
(96 [108, 120] cm) only*

Work 0 (1, 1) rnd even.

NEXT RND: (dec rnd) *Ssk, work to 2 sts before m, k2tog, sl m, work to next m; rep from * once more—4 body sts dec'd.

Legend:

☐	knit
•	purl
○	yo
╱	k2tog
╲	ssk
⋀	sl 2 as if to k2tog, k1, p2sso
▨	no stitch
☐	pattern repeat
⟋⟋	sl 1 st onto cn, hold in back, k1, k1 from cn
⟋⟋	sl 2 sts onto cn, hold in back, k2, k2 from cn
⟋⟋	sl 3 sts onto cn, hold in back, k3, k3 from cn

Rep dec rnd every rnd 1 (0, 0) more time, then every other rnd 4 (4, 1) more time(s)— 286 (312, 338) sts rem; 78 (90, 104) sts for each of back and front; 65 (66, 65) sts each sleeve.

All sizes

234 (260, 286, 312, 338, 364) sts rem; 64 (78, 78, 90, 104, 116) sts for each of back and front; 53 (52, 65, 66, 65, 66) sts each sleeve. Work 1 (1, 1, 1, 7, 6) rnds even, ending with Row 3 of Cable Rib chart, ending last rnd 4 (0, 0, 4, 0, 4) sts before end of rnd.

Remove all markers, work 0 (3, 3, 0, 3, 0) sts, then pm for beg of rnd. Work Rows 1–46 of Yoke chart—126 (140, 154, 168, 182, 196) sts rem.

DEC/BO RND: Work the following rnd, and BO all sts as it is worked: *k1, sl 2 as if to k2tog, k1, p2sso, k1, k2tog; rep from * around.

Finishing

Join Underarms

Place 4 (6, 8, 6, 8, 6) underarm sts from body onto smaller dpn and 4 (6, 8, 6, 8, 6) corresponding underarm sts from sleeve onto another smaller dpn. With WS facing, using yarn tail and the three-needle method (see Glossary), BO underarm sts. Rep for second underarm.

Weave in loose ends. Block to measurements.

Row Gauge

After knitting a swatch for a piece, knitters often check the stitch gauge but not the row gauge. Making sure that you get not only the correct stitch gauge but also the correct row gauge is very important when working this piece. The waist and yoke shaping will fit best when the row gauge is as stated in the pattern.

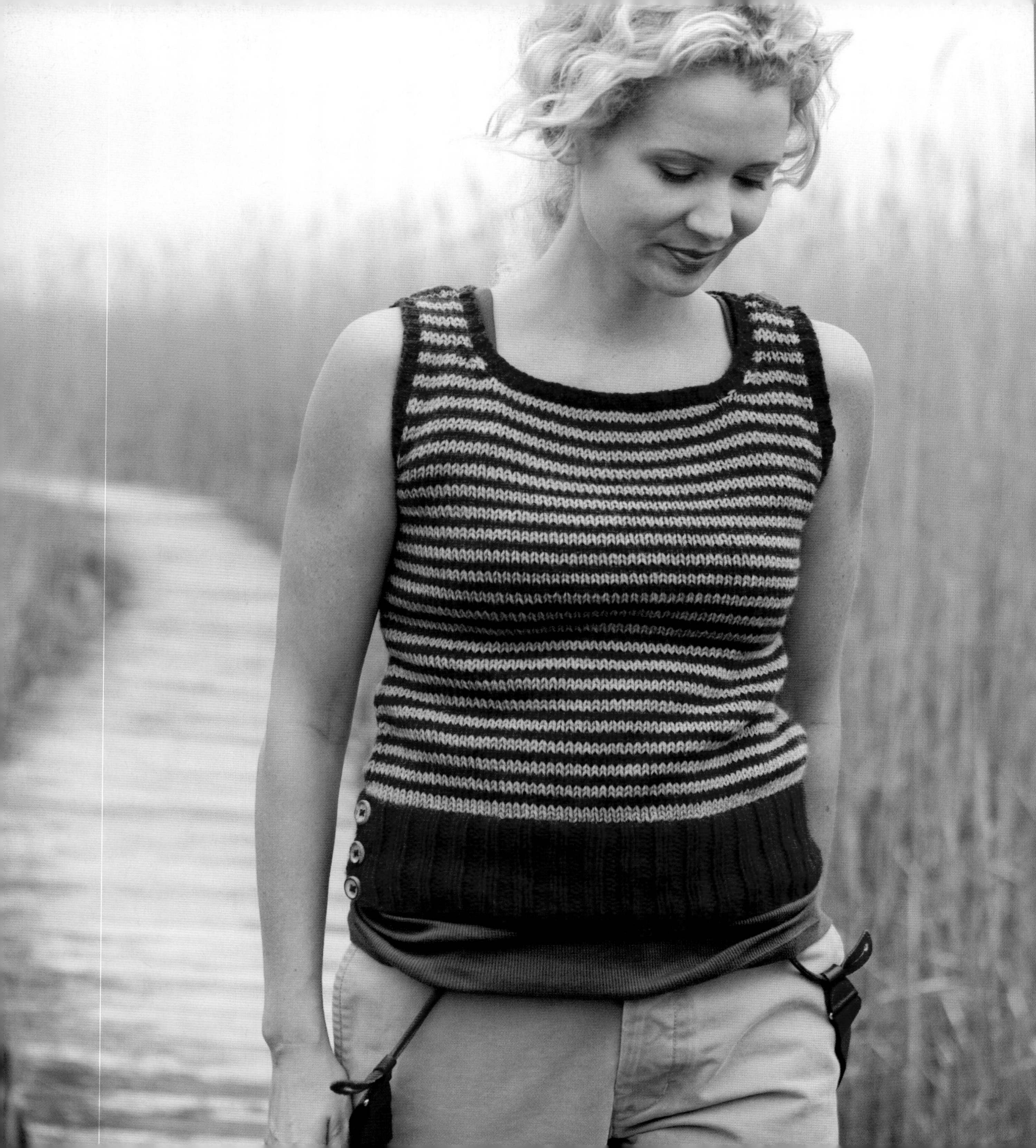

lewiston
STRIPED VEST

DESIGNER

Melissa LaBarre

The classic striped vest goes modern with high-contrast stripes. A button closure at one side of the bottom ribbing and decorative button tabs at the shoulders lend a nautical air. Choose a size close to your measurements to wear this on its own or make a slightly larger size for a versatile layer.

finished size

34 (38, 42, 46½, 50½, 55)" (86.5 [96.5, 106.5, 118, 128.5, 139.5] cm) bust circumference; vest shown measures 34" (86.5 cm).

YARN

Worsted (Medium #4).

shown here: Cascade 220 Heathers (100% wool; 220 yd [201 m]/100 g): #9489 red (MC), 2 (2, 3, 3, 3, 3) skeins, and #9452 blue (CC), 1 (1, 2, 2, 2, 2) skeins.

NEEDLES

U.S. size 7 (4.5 mm): 24" (60 cm) circular (cir). U.S. size 5 (3.75 mm): 29" (73.5 cm) cir and set of 4 or 5 double-pointed (dpn). Adjust needle size if necessary to obtain the correct gauge.

NOTIONS

Five ¾" (2 cm) buttons; marker (m); tapestry needle.

GAUGE

18 sts and 25 rows = 4" (10 cm) in St st on larger needle.

Front

With CC and larger needle, CO 77 (86, 95, 105, 114, 124) sts. Work 2 rows in St st. Change to MC and work 2 rows in St st. Cont in St st, alternating colors every 2 rows, until piece measures 2½" (6.5 cm) from CO, ending with a WS row.

Maintaining stripe patt as established, shape waist as foll:

NEXT ROW: (RS; dec row) K1, ssk, knit to last 3 sts, k2tog, k1—2 sts dec'd.

Rep dec row every 6th row 2 more times—71 (80, 89, 99, 108, 118) sts rem.

Work even in patt for 1" (2.5 cm), ending with a WS row.

NEXT ROW: (RS; inc row) K1, k1f&b, knit to last 2 sts, k1f&b, k1—2 sts inc'd.

Rep inc row every 6th row 2 more times—77 (86, 95, 105, 114, 124) sts.

Work even in stripe patt until piece measures 10½" (26.5 cm) from CO, ending with a WS row.

Shape Armhole

Cont in patt, BO 4 (4, 6, 6, 8, 8) sts at beg of next 2 rows—69 (78, 83, 93, 98, 108) sts rem.

NEXT ROW: (RS; dec row) K1, sssk (see Glossary), knit to last 4 sts, k3tog, k1—4 sts dec'd.

NEXT ROW: Purl.

Rep last 2 rows once more—61 (70, 75, 85, 90, 100) sts rem.

Work even in patt until armholes measure 4 (4½, 5, 5½, 6, 6½)" (10 [11.5, 12.5, 14, 15, 16.5] cm), ending with a WS row.

Shape Neck

NEXT ROW: (RS) K14, attach a new strand of yarn and BO 33 (42, 47, 57, 62, 72) sts, knit to end—14 sts rem each side.

Work each side separately at the same time.

Work 1 row even.

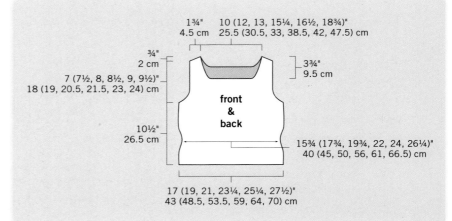

NEXT ROW: (RS) Knit to 4 sts before neck BO, k3tog, k1; on second side, k1, sssk, knit to end—2 sts dec'd each side.

Rep last row every RS row 2 more times—8 sts rem each side.

Work even in patt until armholes measure 7 (7½, 8, 8½, 9, 9½)" (18 [19, 20.5, 21.5, 23, 24] cm), ending with a WS row. BO 4 sts at beg of next 4 rows—no sts rem.

Back

Work as for front until armholes measure 5½ (6, 6½, 7, 7½, 8)" (14 [15, 16.5, 18, 19, 20.5] cm), ending with a WS row, then shape neck as for front. Cont in patt until armholes measure 7 (7½, 8, 8½, 9, 9½)" (18 [19, 20.5, 21.5, 23, 24] cm), ending with a WS row. BO 4 sts at beg of next 4 rows—no sts rem.

Finishing

Sew side seams, being careful to match stripes.

Bottom Ribbing

With MC, RS facing, smaller cir needle, and beg at right side seam, pick up and knit (see Glossary)

153 (161, 169, 177, 185, 193) sts evenly spaced around bottom edge, then use the backward-loop method (see Glossary) to CO 3 sts for button placket—156 (164, 172, 180, 188, 196) sts total. Do not join.

NEXT ROW: (WS; rib patt row) K3, *p2, k2; rep from * to last 5 sts, p5.

Work 2 more rows in rib as established.

NEXT ROW: (RS; buttonhole row) K2tog, yo, work in rib patt to end.

Cont in rib patt and at the same time rep buttonhole row every 8th row 2 more times.

Work 3 rows in rib patt. BO all sts in patt.

Sew buttons to button placket opposite buttonholes.

Shoulder Tabs

With MC, smaller needle, and RS facing, pick up and knit 7 sts from BO edge of left front shoulder. Beg with a WS row, work 3 rows in St st.

ROW 4: (RS) Ssk, k3, k2tog—5 sts rem.

ROWS 5, 7, AND 9: Purl.

ROW 6: (buttonhole row) K2, yo, k2tog, k1.

ROW 8: Ssk, k1, k2tog—3 sts rem.

ROW 10: Sl 2 as if to k2tog, k1, p2sso—1 st rem.

Break yarn and draw through rem st. Rep for right front shoulder.

Sew shoulder seams. Sew buttons to back shoulders opposite buttonholes.

Armhole Edging

With MC, dpn, RS facing, and beg at underarm seam, pick up and knit 92 (96, 100, 104, 108, 112) sts evenly spaced around opening. Place marker (pm) and join for working in the rnd. Work 2 rnds in k2, p2 rib. BO all sts in patt.

Rep for other armhole.

Neck Edging

With MC, dpn, RS facing, and beg at center back neck, pick up and knit 120 (128, 136, 144, 152, 160) sts evenly spaced around neck opening. Pm and join for working in the rnd. Work 2 rnds in k2, p2 rib. BO all sts in patt.

Weave in loose ends.

Carrying Yarn Up the Sides for Stripes

In short striping sequences (such as the two-row pattern of this vest), the unused color yarns can be carried up the side the whole time. Rather than cutting the yarn after each row and leaving lots of ends to weave in, you can simply drop the last yarn worked and pick up the next. When the pieces are seamed, the floats will be hidden inside. When picking up the next color, be careful not to pull the yarn too tightly on the first stitch, because the yarn will need a little slack as it is carried along the side. Pulling too tightly could make the edge stitches bunch up, making for a piece that is awkward to seam.

middlefield
PULLOVER

DESIGNER
Melissa La Barre

This pullover makes a perfect everyday sweater. Worked in two directions, it leaves lots of opportunities for customization—try on the sweater as you work to find the perfect sleeve and body lengths, then customize the neckline to a perfect height for as much or little coverage as you choose.

finished size

34 (38, 42, 46¼, 49¾)" (86.5 [96.5, 106.5, 117.5, 126.5] cm) bust circumference; sweater shown measures 34" (86.5 cm).

YARN

Worsted (Medium #4).

shown here: Louet Riverstone Light Worsted (100% wool; 193 yd [176 m]/100 g): #35 mustard, 4 (5, 6, 6, 7) skeins.

NEEDLES

U.S. size 8 (5 mm): 24" (60 cm) circular (cir) and set of 4 or 5 double-pointed (dpn). Adjust needle size if necessary to obtain the correct gauge.

NOTIONS

3 markers (m); stitch holders or waste yarn; three ⅝" (1.5 cm) buttons; tapestry needle.

GAUGE

18 sts and 24 rows = 4" (10 cm) in St st.

Sweater

Mid Yoke

With cir needle and using the long-tail method (see Glossary), CO 141 (153, 171, 192, 198) sts. Place marker (pm) and join for working in the rnd, being careful not to twist sts.

Knit 3 rnds.

Purl 4 rnds.

Knit 2 rnds.

NEXT RND: (inc rnd) *K2, k1f&b; rep from * to end of rnd—188 (204, 228, 256, 264) sts.

Purl 4 rnds.

Knit 2 rnds.

NEXT RND: (inc rnd) *K3, k1f&b; rep from * to end of rnd—235 (255, 285, 320, 330) sts.

Purl 4 rnds.

Divide for Body and Sleeves

K36 (39, 43, 48, 50), place next 45 (50, 56, 64, 65) sts on holder for sleeve, use the backward-loop method (see Glossary) to CO 2 (4, 4, 4, 6) sts for underarm, pm, CO 2 (4, 4, 4, 6) sts for underarm, k73 (77, 87, 96, 100) for front, place next 45 (50, 56, 64, 65) sts on holder for sleeve, CO 2 (4, 4, 4, 6) sts for underarm, pm, CO 2 (4, 4, 4, 6) sts for underarm, k36 (39, 43, 48, 50)—153 (171, 189, 208, 224) sts rem for body.

Body

NEXT RND: [P2, k2] 5 times, p2, k16 (21, 25, 30, 34), sl m, k16 (21, 25, 30, 34), [p2, k2] 5 times, p2, knit to end of rnd.

Work sts as they appear until piece measures 1" (2.5 cm) from underarm.

Shape Waist

NEXT RND: (dec rnd) *Work in patt to 2 sts before m, ssk, sl m, k2tog; rep from * once more, work in patt to end of rnd—4 sts dec'd.

Rep dec rnd every 7th rnd 3 more times—137 (155, 173, 192, 208) sts rem.

Work even for 1" (2.5 cm).

NEXT RND: (inc rnd) *Work in patt to 1 st before m, M1R (see Glossary), k1, sl m, k1, M1L; rep from * once more, work in patt to end—4 sts inc'd.

Rep inc rnd every 7th rnd 3 more times—153 (171, 189, 208, 224) sts.

Cont in patt as established until piece measures 13" (33 cm) from underarm.

Hem

NEXT RND: (turning rnd) Purl.

Knit 5 rnds.

Sew hem as foll: Fold lower edge of sweater to WS at turning rnd. With yarn threaded on a tapestry needle, sew live sts to corresponding sts on inside of sweater.

Sleeve

Place 45 (50, 56, 64, 65) held sleeve sts onto dpn. Beg at center of underarm, pick up and knit (see Glossary) 3 (5, 5, 5, 7) sts in CO sts, k45 (50, 56, 64, 65), pick up and knit 3 (5, 5, 5, 7) sts in CO sts, pm and join for working in the rnd—51 (60, 66, 74, 79) sts total.

Work in St st until piece measures 10" (25.5 cm) from underarm.

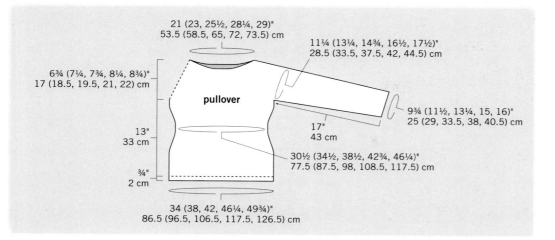

21 (23, 25½, 28¼, 29)"
53.5 (58.5, 65, 72, 73.5) cm

11¼ (13¼, 14¾, 16½, 17½)"
28.5 (33.5, 37.5, 42, 44.5) cm

6¾ (7¼, 7¾, 8¼, 8¾)"
17 (18.5, 19.5, 21, 22) cm

pullover

9¾ (11½, 13¼, 15, 16)"
25 (29, 33.5, 38, 40.5) cm

13"
33 cm

17"
43 cm

30½ (34½, 38½, 42¾, 46¼)"
77.5 (87.5, 98, 108.5, 117.5) cm

¾"
2 cm

34 (38, 42, 46¼, 49¾)"
86.5 (96.5, 106.5, 117.5, 126.5) cm

NEXT RND: (dec rnd) K1, k2tog, knit to last 3 sts, ssk, k1—2 sts dec'd.

Rep dec rnd every 7th rnd 2 more times—45 (54, 60, 68, 73) sts rem.

Knit 1 rnd.

NEXT RND: Dec 1 (2, 0, 0, 1) st(s) evenly spaced around—44 (52, 60, 68, 72) sts rem.

Work in k2, p2 rib until piece measures 17" (43 cm) from underarm. BO all sts in rib.

Ribbed Yoke

With RS facing, cir needle, and beg at left shoulder, pick up and knit 141 (153, 171, 189, 195) sts evenly spaced around neck opening. Do not join; work back and forth in rows.

NEXT ROW: (WS) K3, *p2, k4; rep from * to end of row.

Work 2 more rows even in patt.

Shape back neck

Work short-rows (see Glossary) as foll:

SHORT-ROW 1: (RS) Work to last 16 sts, wrap next st, turn.

SHORT-ROW 2: (WS) Work 42 (48, 54, 66, 66) sts in patt, wrap next st, turn.

Adding Short-rows to Raise the Back of the Neck in Seamless Knits

Short-rows are a great technique for adding length to a specific part of a garment without adding length to the entire piece. Short-rows are made by working only some of the stitches in a row and using a wrap-and-turn technique to avoid holes in the knitting. Adding a couple of short-rows to the back neck of a raglan or yoke sweater will lift the back neck up higher, allowing the front neck to drop and sit more comfortably around the neck.

To raise a back neck for a custom fit, begin by deciding where you would like a section of the piece to have a little extra room, which may be just at the center back of the neck or from shoulder to shoulder, and mark the beginning and end with stitch markers. (For general directions on how to work the stitches of a short-row, see the Glossary.)

After defining the area with markers, work past the first short-row marker on the next row to one stitch before the second short-row marker. Wrap the next stitch and turn, work back to one stitch before the next marker, wrap the next stitch and turn, and work to end of row. When you come to wrapped stitches, work the wrapped stitch together with its wrap. Continue working in the previously established pattern; when you come across the other wrapped stitch on the first row, don't forget to work it together with its wrap. Repeat the short row after about 2" (5 cm). Try your sweater on at any point to check whether the neckline feels comfortable and add another short-row section if it's needed.

SHORT-ROW 3: Work 41 (47, 53, 65, 65) sts in patt, wrap next st, turn.

SHORT-ROW 4: Work 40 (46, 52, 64, 64) sts in patt, wrap next st, turn.

NEXT ROW: (RS) Work to end of row, working wraps tog with wrapped sts.

NEXT ROW: Work to end of row, working rem wraps tog with wrapped sts.

Work 2 more rows even in patt.

NEXT ROW: (RS; dec row) P3, k2tog, *ssk, p2, k2tog; rep from * to last 4 sts, ssk, p2—95 (103, 115, 127, 131) sts rem.

NEXT ROW: (WS) *K2, p2; rep from * to last 3 sts, k3.

Cont in newly established rib patt until piece measures 6¾ (7¼, 7¾, 8¼, 8¾)" (17 [18.5, 19.5, 21, 22] cm) from underarm at center back, ending with a WS row. BO all sts in patt.

Finishing

Buttonhole Tab

With RS facing and beg at BO edge, pick up and knit 13 sts along back edge of ribbed yoke. Purl 1 row.

NEXT ROW: (RS) K1, k2tog, yo, k2, k2tog, yo, k2, k2tog, yo, k2.

Purl 1 row. With RS facing, BO all sts pwise.

Sew buttons to front edge of yoke opposite buttonholes. Weave in loose ends. Block to measurements.

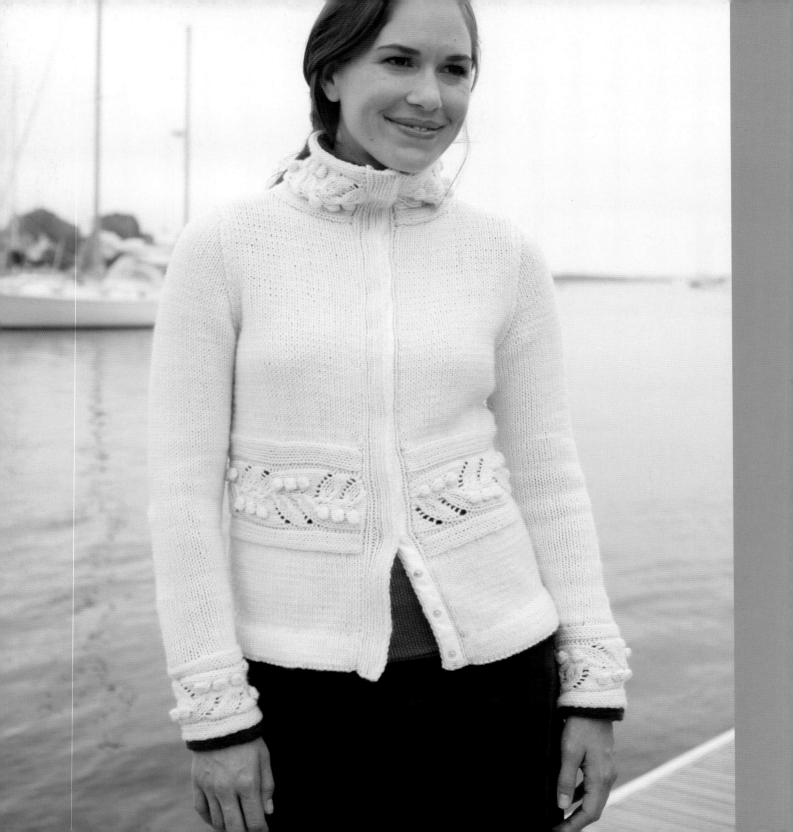

cranston
COAT

DESIGNER
Cecily Glowik MacDonald

Colorful stockinette panels line the lace areas of this elegant coat. The soft cashmere linings keep the wind out while brightening your winter wardrobe—in the coldest weather, a little color is a special pleasure. By lining small areas at the cuffs, waist, and collar, this design uses a small amount of luxury yarn to maximum effect.

finished size
37½ (41½, 45, 49, 52½)" (95 [105.5, 114.5, 124.5, 133.5] cm) bust circumference, closed; jacket shown measures 37½" (95 cm).

YARN
Worsted (Medium #4) and DK (Light #3).

shown here: Valley Yarns Amherst (100% merino; 109 yd [100 m]/50 g): natural (MC), 11 (12, 13, 14, 15) balls.

Classic Elite Marly (100% cashmere; 190 yd [174 m]/50 g): #MRL53 berry (CC), 2 (2, 3, 3, 3) hanks.

NEEDLES
U.S. sizes 6 and 7 (4 and 4.5 mm). U.S. size 8 (5 mm): 29" (73.5 cm) circular (cir). Adjust needle size if necessary to obtain the correct gauge.

NOTIONS
Large stitch holders or waste yarn; 1 yd [1 m] snap tape; matching sewing thread and sewing needle; tapestry needle.

GAUGE
17 sts and 25 rows = 4" (10 cm) in St st with MC on largest needle.

19 sts and 28 rows= 4" (10 cm) in St st with CC on middle-size needles.

Body

Center Panel

With MC and largest needle, CO 25 sts.

NEXT ROW: K1, work Row 1 of Lace and Bobble chart to last st, k1.

Cont in patt, keeping first and last st in St st, until piece measures about 33 (37, 41, 45, 49)" (84 [94, 104, 114.5, 124.5] cm) from CO, ending with Row 12 or 24 of chart. BO all sts in patt.

Bottom

With MC, largest needle, and RS facing, pick up and knit (see Glossary) 154 (170, 186, 202, 218) sts evenly spaced along left edge of center panel. Work even in St st until piece measures 5½" (14 cm) from pick-up row, ending with a RS row.

NEXT ROW: (WS; turning row) Knit.

Hem

NEXT ROW: (RS; dec row) *K9, k2tog; rep from * to last 0 (5, 10, 4, 9) sts, knit to end—140 (155, 170, 184, 199) sts rem.

Work even in St st until piece measures 1½" (3.8 cm) from turning row, ending with a WS row. BO all sts kwise.

Top

With MC, largest needle, and RS facing, pick up and knit 154 (170, 186, 202, 218) sts evenly spaced along right edge of center panel. Work even in St st until piece measures 5 (4½, 4, 3½, 3)" (12.5 [11.5, 10, 9, 7.5] cm) from pick-up row, ending with a WS row.

Divide Back and Fronts

NEXT ROW: K32 (36, 39, 43, 47) for right front, BO 10 (10, 12, 12, 12) sts, k70 (78, 84, 92, 100) for back, BO 10 (10, 12, 12, 12) sts, k32 (36, 39, 43, 47) for left front. Place sts for right and left front on holders or waste yarn.

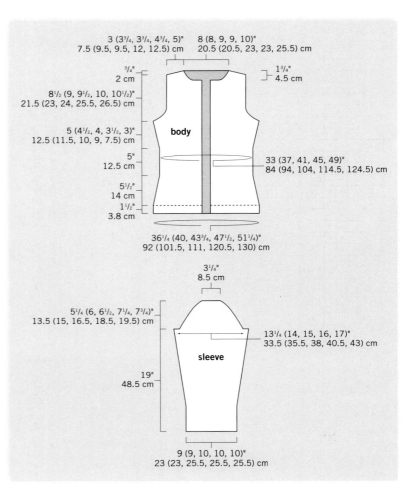

Back

With WS facing, attach MC to 70 (78, 84, 92, 100) back sts. Work 1 WS row even in St st.

Shape Armholes

NEXT ROW: (RS; dec row) K1, ssk, knit to last 3 sts, k2tog, k1—2 sts dec'd.

Rep dec row every RS row 4 (5, 6, 6, 7) more times—60 (66, 70, 78, 84) sts rem. Work even until armholes measure 8½ (9, 9½, 10, 10½)" (21.5 [23, 24, 25.5, 26.5] cm), ending with a WS row.

lace and bobble

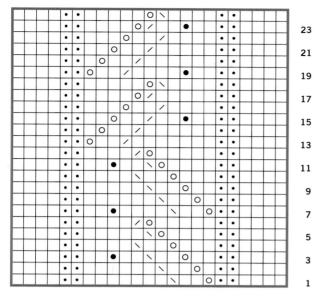

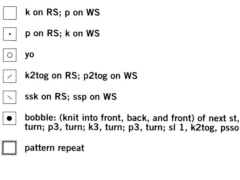

☐	k on RS; p on WS
·	p on RS; k on WS
o	yo
╱	k2tog on RS; p2tog on WS
╲	ssk on RS; ssp on WS
●	bobble: (knit into front, back, and front) of next st, turn; p3, turn; k3, turn; p3, turn; sl 1, k2tog, psso
☐	pattern repeat

Shape Shoulders

BO 6 (8, 8, 10, 10) sts at beg of next 2 rows—48 (50, 54, 58, 64) sts rem. BO 7 (8, 8, 10, 11) sts at beg of foll 2 rows—34 (34, 38, 38, 42) sts rem. BO all sts.

Left Front

Place 32 (36, 39, 43, 47) held left front sts onto largest needle. With WS facing, attach MC. Work 1 WS row even in St st.

Shape Armhole

NEXT ROW: (RS; dec row) K1, ssk, knit to end—1 st dec'd. Rep dec row every RS row 4 (5, 6, 6, 7) more times—27 (30, 32, 36, 39) sts rem.

Work even until armhole measures 7½ (8, 8½, 9, 9½)" (19 [20.5, 21.5, 23, 24] cm), ending with a RS row.

Shape Neck

NEXT ROW: (WS) BO 12 (12, 14, 14, 16) sts at beg of row—15 (18, 18, 22, 23) sts rem.

NEXT ROW: (RS; dec row) Knit to last 3 sts, k2tog, k1—1 st dec'd.

Rep dec row every RS row once more—13 (16, 16, 20, 21) sts rem. Work 3 rows even.

Shape Shoulder

BO 6 (8, 8, 10, 10) sts at beg of next RS row—7 (8, 8, 10, 11) sts rem. Work 1 WS row even. BO all sts.

Right Front

Place 32 (36, 39, 43, 47) held right front sts onto largest needle. With WS facing, attach MC. Work 1 WS row even in St st.

Shape Armhole

NEXT ROW: (RS; dec row) Knit to last 3 sts, k2tog, k1—1 st dec'd.

Rep dec row every RS row 4 (5, 6, 6, 7) more times—27 (30, 32, 36, 39) sts rem. Work even until armhole measures 7½ (8, 8½, 9, 9½)" (19 [20.5, 21.5, 23, 24] cm), ending with a WS row.

Shape Neck

BO 12 (12, 14, 14, 16) sts at beg of next row—15 (18, 18, 22, 23) sts rem. Work 1 WS row even.

NEXT ROW: (RS; dec row) K1, ssk, knit to end—1 st dec'd.

Rep dec row every RS row once more—13 (16, 16, 20, 21) sts rem. Work 2 rows even.

Shape Shoulder

BO 6 (8, 8, 10, 10) sts at beg of next WS row—7 (8, 8, 10, 11) sts rem. Work 1 RS row even. BO all sts.

Sleeves

Cuff

With MC and largest needle, CO 23 sts. Rep Rows 1–24 of Lace and Bobble chart until piece measures 9 (9, 10, 10, 10)" (23 [23, 25.5, 25.5, 25.5] cm) from CO, ending with a WS row. BO all sts in patt.

Sleeve

With MC, largest needle, and RS facing, pick up and knit 38 (38, 42, 42, 42) sts evenly spaced along right edge of cuff. Work even in St st for 3 rows.

Shape Sleeve

NEXT ROW: (RS; inc row) K1, M1L (see Glossary), knit to last st, M1R (see Glossary), k1—2 sts inc'd.

Rep inc row every 4th row 0 (0, 0, 0, 3) more times, every 6th row 0 (1, 1, 9, 11) time(s), every 8th row 1 (9, 9, 3, 0) time(s), then every 10th row 7 (0, 0, 0, 0) times—56 (60, 64, 68, 72) sts. Work even until piece measures 19" (48.5 cm) from farthest edge of cuff panel, ending with a WS row.

Shape Cap

BO 5 (5, 6, 6, 6) sts at beg of next 2 rows—46 (50, 52, 56, 60) sts rem.

NEXT ROW: (RS; dec row) K1, ssk, knit to last 3 sts, k2tog, k1—2 sts dec'd.

Rep dec row every RS row 6 (7, 7, 8, 10) more times, every 4th row 1 (1, 2, 2, 2) time(s), then every RS row 6 (7, 7, 8, 8) times—18 sts rem. BO 2 sts at beg of next 2 rows—14 sts rem. BO all sts.

Collar

With MC and largest needle, CO 23 sts. Rep Rows 1–24 of Lace and Bobble chart until piece measures 19 (19, 21, 21, 23)" (48.5 [48.5, 53.5, 53.5, 58.5] cm) from CO, ending with a WS row. BO all sts in patt.

Finishing

Block pieces to measurements.

Sew shoulder seams. Sew in sleeves. Sew left edge of collar evenly around neck opening. With MC threaded on a tapestry needle, turn hem to WS along turning row and sew in place.

Lining

Sleeve Cuff Lining

With CC and middle-size needles, CO 24 sts. Work even in St st until piece measures 9 (9, 10, 10, 10)" (23 [23, 25.5, 25.5, 25.5] cm) from CO. BO all sts. Rep for second cuff lining.

Center Panel Lining

With CC and middle-size needles, CO 25 sts. Work even in St st until piece measures 33 (37, 41, 45, 49)" (84 [94, 104, 114.5, 124.5] cm) from CO. BO all sts.

Collar Lining

With CC and middle-size needles, CO 24 sts. Work even in St st until piece measures 19 (19, 21, 21, 23)" (48.5 [48.5, 53.5, 53.5, 58.5] cm) from CO. BO all sts.

Block lining pieces.

With WS tog and MC threaded on a tapestry needle, sew linings to inside of corresponding panels. Use mattress stitch (see Glossary) at top of neck and open ends of sleeve cuffs for a neat edge.

Sew sleeve seams.

Snap Bands

Left Band

With MC and smallest needles, CO 11 sts.

ROW 1: (RS) *K1, p1; rep from * to last st, k1.

ROW 2: Sl 1 pwise with yarn in front (wyf), *k1, p1; rep from * to end.

Rep Rows 1 and 2, using mattress st to sew band onto edge of left front as you work, until band measures the same length as left front from turning row to top of collar. BO all sts in rib.

Right Band

With MC and smallest needles, CO 11 sts.

ROW 1: (RS) Sl 1 pwise with yarn in back (wyb), *p1, k1; rep from * to end.

ROW 2: *P1, k1; rep from * to last st, p1.

Rep Rows 1 and 2, using mattress st to sew band onto edge of right front as you work, until band measures the same length as right front from turning row to top of collar. BO all sts in rib.

With sewing needle and matching thread, sew one piece of snap tape to RS of left front band and other piece to WS of right front band.

Weave in loose ends.

montague
BULKY LACE VEST

DESIGNER
Melissa LaBarre

The thick, softly spun yarn of this vest provides a warm, insulating layer, but an airy lace pattern keeps a potentially bulky knit from feeling too heavy and stifling. Use a favorite shawl or stick pin to close the fronts, keeping the breezes at bay.

finished size

33½ (38, 42, 46½, 51)" (85 [96.5, 106.5, 118, 129.5] cm) bust circumference; vest shown measures 33½" (85 cm).

YARN

Bulky (Super Bulky #6).

shown here: Tahki Montana (100% wool; 130 yd [119 m]/100 g): #002 bark, 4 (5, 5, 6, 6) skeins.

NEEDLES

U.S. size 13 (9 mm): 32" (80 cm) circular (cir). U.S. size 10 (6 mm): 40" (100 cm) cir. Adjust needle size if necessary to obtain the correct gauge.

NOTIONS

4 markers (m); tapestry needle.

GAUGE

11 sts and 15 rows = 4" (10 cm) in St st on larger needle.

11 sts and 15 rows = 4" (10 cm) in lace patt on larger needle.

Back

With larger needle, CO 46 (52, 58, 64, 70) sts. Do not join.

ROW 1: (RS; set-up row) K3, p1 (3, 5, 7, 9), place marker (pm), work Row 1 of Back chart, pm, p1 (2, 3, 4, 5), k2, p1 (2, 3, 4, 5), pm, work Row 1 of Back chart, pm, p1 (3, 5, 7, 9), k3.

ROW 2: P3, k1 (3, 5, 7, 9), slip marker (sl m), work Row 2 of Back chart, sl m, k1 (2, 3, 4, 5), p2, k1 (2, 3, 4, 5), sl m, work Row 2 of Back chart, sl m, k1 (3, 5, 7, 9), p3.

Work in patt as established until piece measures 8" (20.5 cm) from CO, ending with a WS row.

Shape Waist

NEXT ROW: (RS; dec row) K2, ssk, work in patt to last 4 sts, k2tog, k2—44 (50, 56, 62, 68) sts rem.

Work even in patt for 1" (2.5 cm), ending with a WS row.

NEXT ROW: (RS; dec row) K1, ssk, work in patt to last 3 sts, k2tog, k1—42 (48, 54, 60, 66) sts rem.

Work even in patt for 2" (5 cm), ending with a WS row.

NEXT ROW: (RS; inc row) K2, M1L (see Glossary), work in patt to last 2 sts, M1R (see Glossary), k2—44 (50, 56, 62, 68) sts.

NEXT ROW: (WS) P3, work in patt to last 3 sts, p3.

Work even in patt for 1" (2.5 cm), ending with a WS row.

NEXT ROW: (RS; inc row) K3, M1L, work in patt to last 3 sts, M1R, k3—46 (52, 58, 64, 70) sts.

back

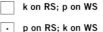

left front   right front

- k on RS; p on WS
- · p on RS; k on WS
- ○ yo
- ╱ k2tog
- ╲ ssk
- ⋏ k3tog
- ⋌ sssk
- ☐ pattern repeat

NEXT ROW: (WS) P3, k1, work in patt to last 4 sts, k1, p3.

Work even in patt until piece measures 14½" (37 cm) from CO, ending with a WS row.

Shape Armholes

BO 4 (6, 8, 10, 12) sts at beg of next 2 rows—38 (40, 42, 44, 46) sts rem.

Cont in patt until armholes measure 7½ (8, 8½, 9, 9½)" (19 [20.5, 21.5, 23, 24] cm), ending with a WS row. BO 2 sts at beg of next 2 rows—34 (36, 38, 40, 42) sts rem. BO 5 sts at beg of next 2 rows—24 (26, 28, 30, 32) sts rem. BO all sts.

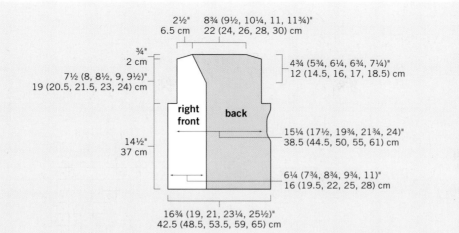

2½"
6.5 cm

8¾ (9½, 10¼, 11, 11¾)"
22 (24, 26, 28, 30) cm

¾"
2 cm

7½ (8, 8½, 9, 9½)"
19 (20.5, 21.5, 23, 24) cm

right front

back

4¾ (5¾, 6¼, 6¾, 7¼)"
12 (14.5, 16, 17, 18.5) cm

15¼ (17½, 19¾, 21¾, 24)"
38.5 (44.5, 50, 55, 61) cm

14½"
37 cm

6¼ (7¾, 8¾, 9¾, 11)"
16 (19.5, 22, 25, 28) cm

16¾ (19, 21, 23¼, 25½)"
42.5 (48.5, 53.5, 59, 65) cm

Left Front

CO 17 (21, 24, 27, 30) sts. Do not join.

ROW 1: (RS; set-up row) K3, p1 (3, 5, 7, 9), pm, work Row 1 of Left Front chart, pm, p1 (3, 4, 5, 6), k2.

ROW 2: P2, k1 (3, 4, 5, 6), work Row 2 of Left Front chart, k1 (3, 5, 7, 9), p3.

Work in patt as established until piece measures 14½" (37 cm) from CO, ending with a WS row.

Shape Armhole

NEXT ROW: (RS) BO 4 (6, 8, 10, 12) sts, work in patt to end—13 (15, 16, 17, 18) sts rem.

Work even in patt until armhole measures 3½ (3, 3, 3, 3)" (9 [7.5, 7.5, 7.5, 7.5] cm), ending with a WS row.

Shape Neck

NEXT ROW: (RS; dec row) Work in patt to last 3 sts, k2tog, k1—1 st dec'd.

Rep dec row every RS row 5 (7, 8, 9, 10) more times—7 sts rem.

Work even in patt until armhole measures 7½ (8, 8½, 9, 9½)" (19 [20.5, 21.5, 23, 24] cm), ending with a WS row.

Shape Shoulder

NEXT ROW: (RS) BO 2 sts, work in patt to end—5 sts rem. Work 1 WS row even.

BO all sts.

Right Front

CO 17 (21, 24, 27, 30) sts. Do not join.

ROW 1: (RS) K2, p1 (3, 4, 5, 6), pm, work Row 1 of Right Front chart, pm, p1 (3, 5, 7, 9), k3.

ROW 2: P3, k1 (3, 5, 7, 9), work Row 2 of Right Front chart, k1 (3, 4, 5, 6), p2.

Work in patt as established until piece measures 14½" (37 cm) from CO, ending with a RS row.

Shape Armhole

NEXT ROW: (WS) BO 4 (6, 8, 10, 12) sts, work in patt to end—13 (15, 16, 17, 18) sts rem.

Work even in patt until armhole measures 3½ (3, 3, 3, 3)" (9 [7.5, 7.5, 7.5, 7.5] cm), ending with a WS row.

Shape Neck

NEXT ROW: (RS; dec row) K1, ssk, work in patt to end—1 st dec'd.

Rep dec row every RS row 5 (7, 8, 9, 10) more times—7 sts rem.

WORK EVEN in patt until armhole measures 7½ (8, 8½, 9, 9½)" (19 [20.5, 21.5, 23, 24] cm), ending with a RS row.

Shape Shoulder

NEXT ROW: (WS) BO 2 sts, work in patt to end—5 sts rem. Work 1 RS row even.

BO all sts.

Finishing

Block pieces to measurements. With yarn threaded on a tapestry needle, sew side and shoulder seams.

Lower Edging

With RS facing and larger needle, pick up and knit (see Glossary) 16 (20, 23, 26, 29) sts along left front lower edge, 44 (50, 56, 62, 68) sts along back, and 16 (20, 23, 26, 29) sts along right front lower edge—76 (90, 102, 114, 126) sts total. Do not join. Knit 2 rows. With WS facing, BO all sts kwise.

Front Band

With smaller cir needle, RS facing, and beg at bottom of right front edge, pick up and knit 84 (87, 88, 91, 92) sts along right front edge, 24 (26, 28, 30, 32) sts along back neck, and 84 (87, 88, 91, 92) sts along left front edge—192 (200, 204, 212, 216) sts total. Do not join.

ROW 1: (RS) K3, *p2, k2; rep from * to last st, k1.

ROW 2: Work sts as they appear.

Cont in patt as established until piece measures 4" (10 cm) from pick-up row, ending with a WS row. Loosely BO all sts in patt.

Seaming With Roving-style Yarns

Roving-type yarns, which may be called "softly spun" or even "unspun," can be difficult to use for sewing seams. Because the fiber isn't spun tightly or plied, these yarns break easily under the strain of the pulling involved with sewing. Save yourself some aggravation by lightly felting the yarn you'll use for seaming.

Cut a length of yarn you plan to seam with and dampen it with water. Roll the strand of yarn between your hands vigorously to create friction, which locks the fibers together. Allow it to dry. You'll find the yarn sturdier and more durable for seaming.

You could also use a lighter-weight or plied yarn in a similar color for seaming; a lighter-weight yarn will also reduce the bulk at the seams.

windsor
WARMER

DESIGNER
Cecily Glowik MacDonald

A long scarf knitted side to side with buttons and buttonholes along the edges offers a variety of options for wear. Wear it unbuttoned like a traditional scarf or fasten the buttons and wrap it a few times around your head and neck as a cowl. A sophisticated lace pattern and cashmere yarn make this irresistible any way you wear it.

finished size
50" (127 cm) long and 7¼" (18.5 cm) wide.

YARN
DK (Light #3).
shown here: **Classic Elite Marly** (100% cashmere; 190 yd [174 m]/50 g): #MRL76 brown, 2 hanks.

NEEDLES
U.S. size 7 (4.5 mm). Adjust needle size if necessary to obtain the correct gauge.

NOTIONS
Size H/8 (5 mm) crochet hook; five ⅝" (1.5 cm) buttons; tapestry needle.

GAUGE
19 sts and 28 rows = 4" (10 cm) in lace rib patt, after blocking.

Stitch Guide

lace rib pattern
(multiple of 17 sts + 6)

ROW 1: (RS) *P2, k2, p2, k2tog, k3, yo, k1, yo, k3, ssk; rep from * to last 6 sts, p2, k2, p2.

ROW 2 AND ALL WS ROWS: K2, p2, k2, *p11, k2, p2, k2; rep from * to end.

ROW 3: *P2, k2, p2, k2tog, k2, yo, k3, yo, k2, ssk; rep from * to last 6 sts, p2, k2, p2.

ROW 5: *P2, k2, p2, k2tog, k1, yo, k5, yo, k1, ssk; rep from * to last 6 sts, p2, k2, p2.

ROWS 7 AND 9: *P2, k2, p2, k2tog, yo, k1, k2tog, yo, k1, yo, ssk, k1, yo, ssk; rep from * to last 6 sts, p2, k2, p2.

ROW 11: Rep Row 5.

ROW 13: Rep Row 3.

ROW 15: Rep Row 1.

ROW 16: Rep Row 2.

Rep Rows 1–16 for patt.

Warmer

CO 244 sts. Work in k1, p1 rib for 3 rows. Work Lace Rib patt (see Stitch Guide or chart) until piece measures 7" (18 cm) from CO, ending with a RS row. Work in k1, p1 rib for 3 rows. BO all sts in rib.

Finishing

Block piece to measurements.

Buttonband

With crochet hook and RS facing, work 25 sc evenly spaced along left edge of warmer; fasten off. (See Glossary for crochet instructions.)

Button Loops

With crochet hook and RS facing, work 25 sc evenly spaced along right edge of warmer.

NEXT ROW: (WS) Ch 1, sc in first 2 sc, *ch 3, skip 1 sc, sc in next 4 sc; rep from * to last 3 sc, ch 3, skip 1 sc, sc in next 2 sc.

NEXT ROW: Ch 1, sc in first 2 sc, *work 3 sc in ch-space, skip 1 sc, sc in next 3 sc; rep from * to last ch-space, work 3 sc in ch-space, sc in next 2 sc. Fasten off.

Sew buttons to buttonband opposite button loops. Weave in loose ends.

lace rib

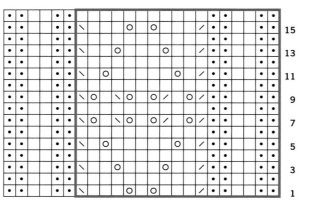

☐	k on RS; p on WS
·	p on RS; k on WS
○	yo
╱	k2tog
╲	ssk
☐	pattern repeat

Working the Long Way

When knitting a scarf from side to side, cast on all the stitches needed for the finished length of the piece. Knitting a piece this way can make it easier to experiment with a stitch pattern, because you get to work the same repeat over a longer section—there's no need for a stitch pattern that can be completed in only a few inches of width. Working the long way also makes working "just one more row" much more significant. Just a few rows, and you're done!

beg	begin(s); beginning	M1	make one (increase)	st	stitch(es)
BO	bind off	p	purl	St st	stockinette stitch
CC	contrasting color	p1f&b	purl into front and back of same stitch	tbl	through back loop
cm	centimeter(s)			tog	together
cn	cable needle	patt(s)	pattern(s)	WS	wrong side
CO	cast on	psso	pass slipped stitch over	wyb	with yarn in back
cont	continue(s); continuing	pwise	purlwise, as if to purl	wyf	with yarn in front
dec(s)	decrease(s); decreasing	rem	remain(s); remaining	yd	yard(s)
dpn	double-pointed needles	rep	repeat(s); repeating	yo	yarnover
foll	follow(s); following	rev St st	reverse stockinette stitch	*	repeat starting point
g	gram(s)	rnd(s)	round(s)	* *	repeat all instructions between asterisks
inc(s)	increase(s); increasing	RS	right side		
k	knit	sl	slip	( )	alternate measurements and/or instructions
k1f&b	knit into the front and back of same stitch	sl st	slip st (slip 1 stitch purlwise unless otherwise indicated)	[ ]	work instructions as a group a specified number of times
kwise	knitwise, as if to knit	ssk	slip 2 stitches knitwise, one at a time, from the left needle to right needle, insert left needle tip through both front loops and knit together from this position (1 stitch decrease)		
m	marker(s)				
MC	main color				
mm	millimeter(s)				

Bind-Offs

Standard Bind-Off

Knit the first stitch, *knit the next stitch (2 stitches on right needle), insert left needle tip into first stitch on right needle (Figure 1) and lift this stitch up and over the second stitch (Figure 2) and off the needle (Figure 3). Repeat from * for the desired number of stitches.

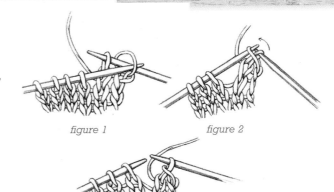

figure 1   *figure 2*

figure 3

Three-Needle Bind-Off

Place the stitches to be joined onto two separate needles and hold the needles parallel so that the right sides of knitting face together. Insert a third needle into the first stitch on each of two needles (Figure 1) and knit them together as one stitch (Figure 2), *knit the next stitch on each needle the same way, then use the left needle tip to lift the first stitch over the second and off the needle (Figure 3). Repeat from * until no stitches remain on first two needles. Cut yarn and pull tail through last stitch to secure.

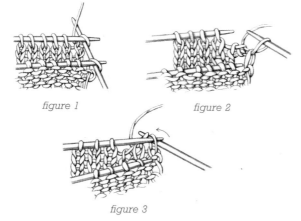

figure 1   figure 2

figure 3

Cables

Slip the designated number of stitches (usually 2 or 3) onto a cable needle, hold the cable needle in front of the work for a left-leaning twist (Figure 1) or in back of the work for a right-leaning twist (Figure 2), work the specified number of stitches from the left needle (usually the same number of stitches that were placed on the cable needle), then work the stitches from the cable needle in the order in which they were placed on the needle (Figure 3).

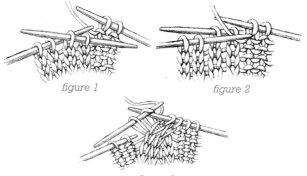

figure 1   figure 2

figure 3

Cast-Ons

Backward-Loop Cast-On

*Loop working yarn and place it on needle backward so that it doesn't unwind. Repeat from *.

Cable Cast-On

If there are no stitches on the needles, make a slipknot of working yarn and place it on the needle, then use the knitted method (see below) to cast on 1 more stitch—2 stitches on needle. Hold needle with working yarn in your left hand. *Insert right needle between the first 2 stitches on left needle (Figure 1), wrap yarn around needle as if to knit, draw yarn through (Figure 2), and place new loop on left needle (Figure 3) to form a new stitch. Repeat from * for the desired number of stitches, always working between the 2 stitches closest to the tip of the left needle.

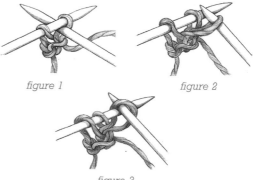

figure 1   figure 2

figure 3

Emily Ocker's Cast-On

This method for casting on for a circle in the round is invisible. Leaving a tail, make a large loop with the yarn. Hold the loop so that the crossing area of the loop is on the top and the tail is off to the left. With a double-pointed knitting needle, *reach inside the loop and pull the yarn coming from the ball through to make a stitch, then take the needle up over the top of the loop and yarn over; repeat from * until you have the desired number of stitches on the needle. Turn and knit one row. If you're casting on an even number of stitches, the sequence ends with a yarnover, and it will be difficult to keep from losing the last stitch. To solve this, pick up 1 extra stitch from the inside and then work these last 2 stitches together on the first row to get back to an even number of stitches. Divide the stitches evenly onto four double-pointed needles.

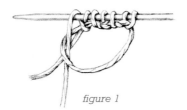

figure 1

Crochet Cast-On

Place a slipknot on a crochet hook. Hold the needle and yarn in your left hand with the yarn under the needle. Place hook over needle, wrap yarn around hook, and pull the loop through the slipknot (Figure 1). *Bring yarn to back under needle tip, wrap yarn around hook, and pull it through loop on hook (Figure 2). Repeat from * until there is one less than the desired number of stitches. Bring the yarn to the back and slip the remaining loop from the hook onto the needle.

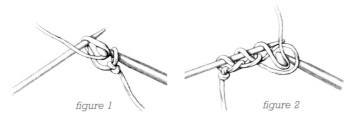

figure 1   *figure 2*

Knitted Cast-On

Make a slipknot of working yarn and place it on the left needle if there are no stitches already there. *Use the right needle to knit the first stitch (or slipknot) on left needle (Figure 1) and place new loop onto left needle to form a new stitch (Figure 2). Repeat from * for the desired number of stitches, always working into the last stitch made.

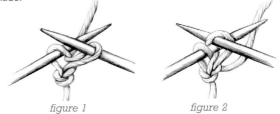

figure 1   *figure 2*

Long-Tail (Continental) Cast-On

Leaving a long tail (about ½" [1.3 cm] for each stitch to be cast on), make a slipknot and place on right needle. Place thumb and index finger of your left hand between the yarn ends so that working yarn is around your index finger and tail end is around your thumb and secure the yarn ends with your other fingers. Hold your palm upward, making a V of yarn (Figure 1). *Bring needle up through loop on thumb (Figure 2), catch first strand around index finger, and go back down through loop on thumb (Figure 3). Drop loop off thumb and, placing thumb back in V configuration, tighten resulting stitch on needle (Figure 4). Repeat from * for the desired number of stitches.

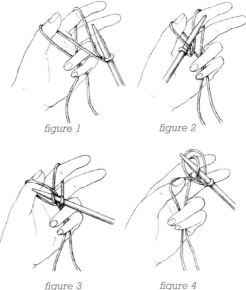

figure 1   *figure 2*

figure 3   *figure 4*

Crochet

Crochet Chain (ch)

Make a slipknot and place it on crochet hook if there isn't a loop already on the hook. *Yarn over hook and draw through loop on hook. Repeat from * for the desired number of stitches. To fasten off, cut yarn and draw end through last loop formed.

Single Crochet (sc)

*Insert hook into the second chain from the hook (or the next stitch), yarn over hook and draw through a loop, yarn over hook (Figure 1), and draw it through both loops on hook (Figure 2). Repeat from * for the desired number of stitches.

figure 1   *figure 2*

Slip-Stitch Crochet (sl st)

*Insert hook into stitch, yarn over hook and draw a loop through both the stitch and the loop already on hook. Repeat from * for the desired number of stitches.

Decreases

Centered Double Decrease (sl 2, k1, p2sso)

Slip 2 stitches together knitwise (Figure 1), knit the next stitch (Figure 2), then pass the slipped stitches over the knitted stitch (Figure 3).

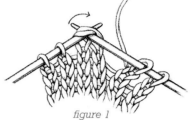

figure 1

figure 2

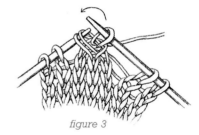

figure 3

Knit 2 Together (k2tog)

Knit 2 stitches together as if they were a single stitch.

Knit 3 Together (k3tog)

Knit 3 stitches together as if they were a single stitch.

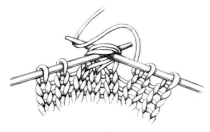

Purl 2 Together (p2tog)

Purl 2 stitches together as if they were a single stitch.

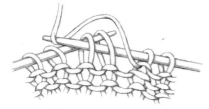

Left-Slant Double Decrease (sl 1, k2tog, psso)

Slip 1 stitch knitwise to right needle, knit the next 2 stitches together (Figure 1), then use the tip of the left needle to lift the slipped stitch up and over the knitted stitches (Figure 2), then off the needle.

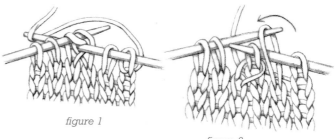

figure 1

figure 2

Slip, Slip, Knit (ssk)

Slip 2 stitches individually knitwise (Figure 1), insert left needle tip into the front of these 2 slipped stitches, and use the right needle to knit them together through their back loops (Figure 2).

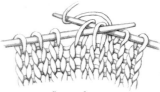

figure 1

figure 2

Slip, Slip, Slip, Knit (sssk)

Slip 3 stitches individually knitwise (Figure 1), insert left needle tip into the front of these 3 slipped stitches, and use the right needle to knit them together through their back loops (Figure 2).

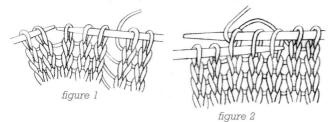

figure 1

figure 2

Slip, Slip, Purl (ssp)

Holding yarn in front, slip 2 stitches individually knitwise (Figure 1), then slip these 2 stitches back onto left needle (they will be turned on the needle) and purl them together through their back loops (Figure 2).

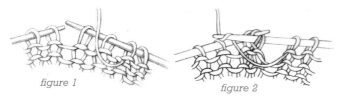

figure 1

figure 2

Embroidery

Lazy Daisy

*Bring threaded needle out of knitted fabric from back to front, form a short loop, and insert needle into background where it came out. Keeping the loop under the needle, bring the needle back out of the background a short distance away (Figure 1), pull loop snug, and insert needle into fabric on far side of loop. Repeat from * for desired number of petals (Figure 2; six petals shown).

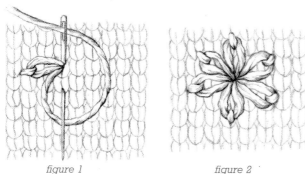

figure 1

figure 2

Gauge

Measuring Gauge

Knit a swatch at least 4" (10 cm) square. Remove the stitches from the needles or bind them off loosely and lay the swatch on a flat surface. Place a ruler over the swatch and count the number of stitches across and number of rows down (including fractions of stitches and rows) in 2" (5 cm) and divide this number by two to get the number of stitches (including fractions of stitches) in one inch. Repeat two or three times on different areas of the swatch to confirm the measurements. If you have more stitches and rows than called for in the instructions, knit another swatch with larger needles; if you have fewer stitches and rows, knit another swatch with smaller needles.

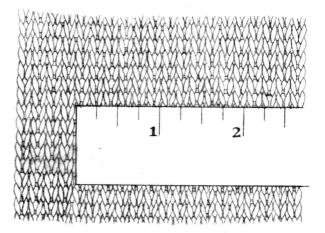

Grafting

Kitchener Stitch

Arrange stitches on two needles so that there is the same number of stitches on each needle. Hold the needles parallel to each other with wrong sides of the knitting together. Allowing about ½" (1.3 cm) per stitch to be grafted, thread matching yarn on a tapestry needle. Work from right to left as follows:

STEP 1. Bring tapestry needle through the first stitch on the front needle as if to purl and leave the stitch on the needle (Figure 1).

STEP 2. Bring tapestry needle through the first stitch on the back needle as if to knit and leave that stitch on the needle (Figure 2).

STEP 3. Bring tapestry needle through the first front stitch as if to knit and slip this stitch off the needle, then bring tapestry needle through the next front stitch as if to purl and leave this stitch on the needle (Figure 3).

STEP 4. Bring tapestry needle through the first back stitch as if to purl and slip this stitch off the needle, then bring tapestry needle through the next back stitch as if to knit and leave this stitch on the needle (Figure 4).

Repeat Steps 3 and 4 until 1 stitch remains on each needle, adjusting the tension to match the rest of the knitting as you go. To finish, bring tapestry needle through the front stitch as if to knit and slip this stitch off the needle, then bring tapestry needle through the back stitch as if to purl and slip this stitch off the needle.

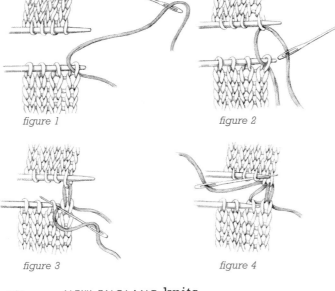

figure 1

figure 2

figure 3

figure 4

I-Cord (also called Knit-Cord)

Using two double-pointed needles, cast on the desired number of stitches (usually 3 to 4). *Without turning the needle, slide stitches to other end of needle, pull the yarn around the back, and knit the stitches as usual. Repeat from * for desired length.

Attached I-Cord

As I-cord is knitted, attach it to the garment as follows: With garment right side facing and using a separate ball of yarn and circular needle, pick up and knit the desired number of stitches along the garment edge. Slide these stitches down the needle so that the first picked-up stitch is near the opposite needle point. With double-pointed needle, cast on the desired number of I-cord stitches. *Knit across the I-cord to the last stitch, then knit the last stitch together with the first picked-up stitch on the garment, and pull the yarn behind the cord. Repeat from * until all picked-up stitches have been used.

Reverse Stockinette Stitch I-Cord (or Knit-Cord)

Work as for regular knit-cord (or I-cord) but purl the stitches instead of knitting them.

Increases

Bar Increase (k1f&b)

Knit into a stitch but leave it on the left needle (Figure 1), then knit through the back loop of the same stitch (Figure 2) and slip the original stitch off the needle (Figure 3).

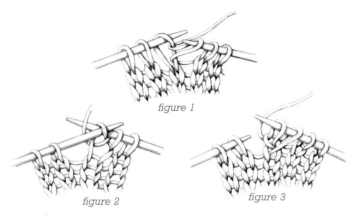

figure 1

figure 2

figure 3

Lifted Increase—Left Slant (LLI)

Insert left needle tip into the back of the stitch below the stitch just knitted (Figure 1), then knit this stitch (Figure 2).

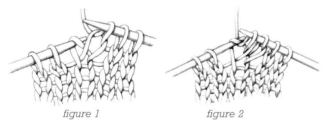

figure 1

figure 2

Lifted Increase—Right Slant (RLI)

Note: If no slant direction is specified, use the right slant.
Knit into the back of the stitch (in the "purl bump") in the row directly below the stitch on the needle (Figure 1), then knit the stitch on the needle (Figure 2), and slip the original stitch off the needle.

figure 1

figure 2

Raised Make One—Left Slant (M1L)

Note: Use the left slant if no direction of slant is specified.
With left needle tip, lift the strand between the last knitted stitch and the first stitch on the left needle from front to back (Figure 1), then knit the lifted loop through the back (Figure 2).

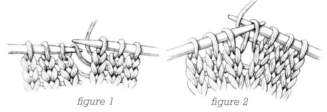

figure 1

figure 2

Raised Make One Purlwise (M1P)

With left needle tip, lift the strand between the needles from front to back, then purl the lifted loop through the front.

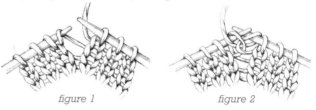

figure 1

figure 2

Raised Make One—Right Slant (M1R)

With left needle tip, lift the strand between the needles from back to front (Figure 1). Knit the lifted loop through the front (Figure 2).

figure 1

figure 2

P1f&b

Purl into a stitch but leave it on the left needle (Figure 1), then purl through the back loop of the same stitch (Figure 2) and slip the original stitch off the needle.

figure 1   *figure 2*

Yarnovers

Backward yarnover

Bring the yarn to the back under the needle, then over the top to the front so that the leading leg of the loop is at the back of the needle.

Yarnover between 2 knit stitches

Wrap the working yarn around the needle from front to back and in position to knit the next stitch.

Yarnover after a knit before a purl

Wrap the working yarn around the needle from front to back, then under the needle to the front again in position to purl the next stitch.

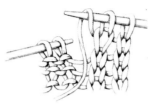

Yarnover between 2 purl sts

Wrap the working yarn around the needle from front to back, then

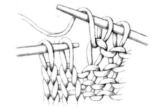

under the needle to the front in position to purl the next stitch.

Yarnover after purl before knit

Wrap the working yarn around the needle from front to back and in position to knit the next stitch.

Knit Through Back Loop (tbl)

Insert right needle through the loop on the back of the left needle from front to back, wrap the yarn around the needle, and pull a loop through while slipping the stitch off the left needle. This is similar to a regular knit stitch, but is worked into the back loop of the stitch instead of the front.

Pick Up and Knit

Pick Up and Knit Along CO or BO Edge

With right side facing and working from right to left, insert the tip of the needle into the center of the stitch below the bind-off or cast-on edge (Figure 1), wrap yarn around needle, and pull through a loop (Figure 2). Pick up 1 stitch for every existing stitch.

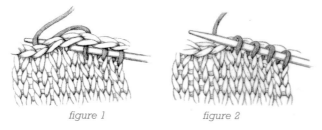

figure 1   *figure 2*

Pick Up and Knit Along Shaped Edge

With right side facing and working from right to left, insert tip of needle between last and second-to-last stitches, wrap yarn around needle, and pull through a loop. Pick up and knit about 3 stitches for every four rows, adjusting as necessary so that picked-up edge lays flat.

Pick Up and Purl

With wrong side of work facing and working from right to left, *insert needle tip under selvedge stitch from the far side to the near side, wrap yarn around needle (Figure 1), and pull a loop through (Figure 2). Repeat from * for desired number of stitches.

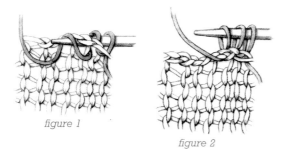

figure 1

figure 2

Seams

Invisible Horizontal Seam

Working with the bound-off edges opposite each other, right sides of the knitting facing you, and working into the stitches just below the bound-off edges, bring threaded tapestry needle out at the center of the first stitch (i.e., go under half of the first stitch) on one side of the seam, then bring needle in and out under the first whole stitch on the other side (Figure 1). *Bring needle into the center of the same stitch it came out of before, then out in the center of the adjacent stitch (Figure 2). Bring needle in and out under the next whole stitch on the other side (Figure 3). Repeat from *, ending with a half-stitch on the first side.

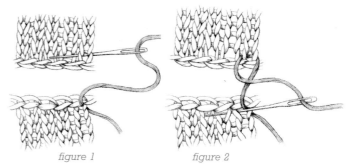

figure 1   *figure 2*

figure 3

Invisible Vertical to Horizontal Seam

With yarn threaded on a tapestry needle, pick up one bar between the first 2 stitches along the vertical edge (Figure 1), then pick up one complete stitch along the horizontal edge (Figure 2). *Pick up the next one or two bars on the first piece, then the next whole stitch on the other piece (Figure 3). Repeat from *, ending by picking up one bar on the vertical edge.

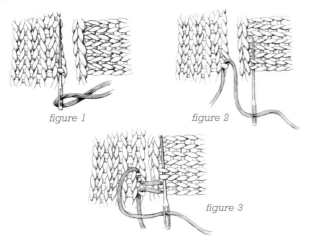

figure 1   figure 2

figure 3

Invisible Vertical Seam (or Mattress Stitch)

Place the pieces to be seamed on a table, right sides facing up. Begin at the lower edge and work upward as follows: Insert threaded needle under one bar between the 2 edge stitches on one piece, then under the corresponding bar plus the bar above it on the other piece (Figure 1). *Pick up the next two bars on the first piece (Figure 2), then the next two bars on the other (Figure 3). Repeat from *, ending by picking up the last bar or pair of bars on the first piece.

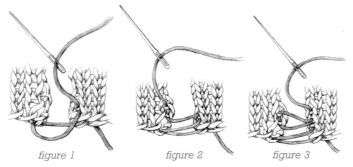

figure 1   figure 2   figure 3

Running Stitch

The most common sewing method. Holding the pieces to be joined together, pass a threaded needle from WS to RS and back, creating stitches that look like a small dashed line of equal lengths on both sides.

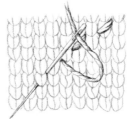

Short-Rows

Short-Rows Knit Side

Work to turning point, slip next stitch purlwise (Figure 1), bring the yarn to the front, then slip the same stitch back to the left needle (Figure 2), turn the work around and bring the yarn in position for the next stitch—1 stitch has been wrapped and the yarn is correctly positioned to work the next stitch. When you come to a wrapped stitch on a subsequent row, hide the wrap by working it together with the wrapped stitch as follows: Insert right needle tip under the wrap (from the front if wrapped stitch is a knit stitch; from the back if wrapped stitch is a purl stitch; Figure 3), then into the stitch on the needle, and work the stitch and its wrap together as a single stitch.

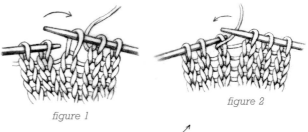

figure 1   figure 2

figure 3

Short-Rows Purl Side

Work to the turning point, slip the next stitch purlwise to the right needle, bring the yarn to the back of the work (Figure 1), return the slipped stitch to the left needle, bring the yarn to the front between the needles (Figure 2), and turn the work so that the knit side is facing—1 stitch has been wrapped and the yarn is correctly positioned to knit the next stitch. To hide the wrap on a subsequent purl row, work to the wrapped stitch, use the tip of the right needle to pick up the wrap from the back, place it on the left needle (Figure 3), then purl it together with the wrapped stitch.

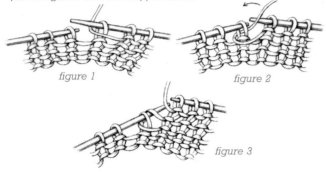

figure 1

figure 2

figure 3

Weave In Loose Ends

Thread the ends on a tapestry needle and trace the path of a row of stitches (Figure 1) or work on the diagonal, catching the back side of the stitches (Figure 2). To reduce bulk, do not weave two ends in the same area. To keep color changes sharp, work the ends into areas of the same color.

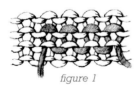

figure 1

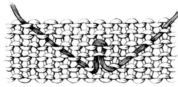

figure 2

CONTRIBUTORS

Carrie Bostick Hoge lives on a lovely green acre in Maine. She stays busy most days working on various knitting, photography, and design projects in her back-yard studio. Carrie is currently working on publishing a little booklet series called "Swatch Diaries," which is available at maddermade.com.

Kate Gagnon Osborn currently resides in Philadelphia but is a true New Englander at heart. Holidays in her native Massachusetts and vacations in Vermont and Maine continue to influence her design aesthetic (and need for warm handknits)! Kate is the co-owner of Kelbourne Woolens, distributor of The Fibre Company yarns, a small artisan yarn company founded in Portland, Maine. She designs regularly for Interweave publications, and her popular free and wholesale pattern lines are available through KelbourneWoolens.com.

Cirilia Rose has many New England attachments, from family ties in the Boston area to college years spent in the Pioneer Valley. She currently works at Berroco in Uxbridge, Massachusetts. She has designed knitwear for Berroco and Classic Elite, and her designs have also appeared in *Knitscene* magazine and *One-Skein Wonders*. For Cirilia, New England style means a healthy respect for timeless staples and an ability to revel in (and dress for) any sort of weather.

Kristen TenDyke is a knit and crochet designer and technical editor. Her designs can be found in publications such as *Vogue Knitting, Interweave Knits, Interweave Crochet, Knit Simple, Knitty,* Classic Elite pattern collections, and more. Kristen has a BFA in graphic design from Massachusetts College of Art and Design, which she uses in her work at Classic Elite Yarns. It also comes in handy to self-publish designs on her website, kristentendyke.com.

RESOURCES

Berroco Inc.
14 Elmdale Rd.
PO Box 367
Uxbridge, MA 01569-0367
(508) 278-2527
fax (508) 278-2461
berroco.com
Ultra Alpaca Fine,
Inca Gold

Bijou Basin Ranch
PO Box 154
Elbert, CO 80106
(303) 601-7544
fax (719) 347-2254
bijoubasinranch.com
50% yak/50% Cormo

Brown Sheep Company Inc.
100662 County Rd.16
Mitchell, NE 69357
(800) 826-9136
fax (308) 635-2143
brownsheep.com
Lamb's Pride Bulky

Cascade Yarns
1224 Andover Pk. E.
Tukwila, WA 98188
(800) 548-1048
fax (206) 574-0436
cascadeyarns.com
Cascade 220

Classic Elite Yarns
122 Western Ave.
Lowell, MA 01851-1434
(978) 453-2837
fax (978) 452-3085
classiceliteyarns.com
Kumara, Marly,
Montera Heathers,
Portland Tweed,
Princess, Silky Alpaca Lace

Debbie Bliss
Distributed by Knitting Fever Inc.
PO Box 336
315 Bayview Ave.
Amityville, NY 11701
(516) 546-3600
fax (516) 546-6871
knittingfever.com
Donegal Chunky Tweed

Fibre Company
Distributed by Kelbourne
Woolens
915 N. 28th St., Second Fl.
Philadelphia, PA 19130
(215) 687-5534
fax (215) 701-5901
kelbournewoolens.com
Canopy Fingering,
Organik

Karabella Yarns
1201 Broadway
New York, NY 10001
(212) 684-2665
fax (646) 935-0588
karabellayarns.com
Soft Tweed

Louet Sales
808 Commerce Park Dr.
Ogdensburg, NY 13669
(800) 897-6444
fax (613) 925-1405
louet.com
Riverstone Light Worsted

Malabrigo
malabrigoyarns.com
Merino Worsted

Manos del Uruguay
Distributed in the United States
by Fairmount Fibers
PO Box 2082
915 N. 28th St.
Philadelphia, PA 19130
(888) 566-9970
fax (215) 235-3498
fairmountfibers.com
Wool Clasica

Reynolds Yarns
Distributed by JCA Inc.
35 Scales LN.
Townsend, MA 01469
(800) 225-6340
fax (978) 597-2632
jcacrafts.com
Lite Lopi, Candide

Rowan
Distributed in the United States
by Westminster Fibers Inc.
165 Ledge St.
Nashua, NH 03060
(800) 445-9276
westminsterfibers.com
Organic Wool Naturally Dyed/
Purelife

St-Denis Yarns
Distributed by Classic Elite
Yarns
122 Western Ave.
Lowell, MA 01851-1434
(978) 453-2837
fax (978) 452-3085
classiceliteyarns.com
stdenisyarns.com
Nordique

Shibui Knits
1101 SW Alder St.
Portland, OR 97205
(503) 595-5898
fax (503) 227-0009
shibuiknits.com
Merino Kid

Tahki Stacy Charles Inc.
70–30 80th St., Bldg. 36
Ridgewood, NY 11385
(800) 338-YARN
fax (718) 326-5017
tahkistacycharles.com
Montana

Valley Yarns
Distributed by Webs
75 Service Center Rd.
Northampton, MA 01060
(800) 367-9327
fax (413) 584-1603
yarn.com
Amherst

Vermont Organic Fiber
Company
52 Seymour St. #A
Middlebury, VT 05753-1115
(802) 388-1344
fax (802) 388-4351
o-wool.com
O-Wool Classic

INDEX

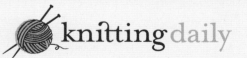